S0-BZU-900

THE ENGLISH RELIGIOUS TRADITION

THE ENGLISH RELIGIOUS TRADITION

SKETCHES
OF ITS INFLUENCE ON CHURCH,
STATE, AND SOCIETY

by

NORMAN SYKES, F.B.A.

Dixie Professor of Ecclesiastical History, and Fellow of Emmanuel College, Cambridge

SCM PRESS LTD
56 BLOOMSBURY STREET
LONDON

εὑρὼν δὲ ἕνα πολύτιμον μαργαρίτην.

'when he had found one pearl of great price'.
(Matt. 13.46)

First published November 1953

Printed in Great Britain by
Northumberland Press Limited
Gateshead on Tyne

CONTENTS

PREFACE

THE following pages owe their origin to an invitation conveyed to me by Mr. E. H. Robertson of the British Broadcasting Corporation to deliver a series of talks in the European Service on the English religious tradition and its influence on the development of Church, State, and Society in England. The execution of the plan was delegated to Marcus Worsley of the B.B.C. European Service, to whom I owe the debt of criticism, suggestion, and counsel in the preparation and delivery of the series. I think however that 'execution' is the *mot juste*. For six months in 1952 he functioned as executioner alike of my written scripts and of my oral delivery. From both functions I benefited greatly; and he should have the credit for what is good in my talks, and I the blame for what is amiss. When the S.C.M. Press honoured me by the suggestion of publishing the talks, I readily agreed, but realized that they must be printed as they stood, with all their imperfections and omissions. I am aware that I have been selective in the choice of topics and of illustrations. It could not be otherwise. But I hope that what I have done may be useful and even interesting to my readers, and may stimulate some to fill in my gaps, and achieve a greater measure of success than I have been able to command.

N.S.

1. THE HERITAGE OF THE MIDDLE AGES

(i) Nationalism

In one of the scenes of Mr. Bernard Shaw's chronicle play *St. Joan*, the author introduces two typical figures of medieval society, an English nobleman and a French bishop; and together they discuss the forces which were making for the downfall of that order and the emergence of the modern world. With characteristic paradox, Mr. Shaw puts into the mouth of the Earl of Warwick his diagnosis of the religious factor. 'It is the protest of the individual soul against the interference of priest or peer between the private man and his God. I should call it Protestantism, if I had to find a name for it.' To this the Bishop of Beauvais replies by identifying its political counterpart as shown in the career of Joan of Arc. 'Call this side of her heresy, Nationalism, if you will. I can find no better name for it.'

The playwright was not interested of course in historical probabilities; and we may well doubt whether even the most far-seeing of English noblemen or French ecclesiastics would have realized at such an early date the nature of the forces which, a century later, were to burst asunder the unity of western Christendom. But there can be no doubt at all that it was the combination of Nationalism and Protestantism which determined the peculiar character of the Reformation in England; and gave birth to that English Religious Tradition, the various aspects and developments of which, during the last four centuries, form the subject of this series of talks.

It must not be supposed however that the Church in England during the central period of the middle ages, that is, the five hundred years roughly dividing the Norman Conquest from the accession of Elizabeth I, differed fundamentally from the Church in the other states of western Europe. It was a mistake of an older generation of historians, inspired partly by patriotic zeal and partly by an imperfect historical perspective, to try and read back into the middle ages an independence of Rome on the part of our forefathers, of which they became conscious only after the Reformation. It is true that the planting of Christianity in these islands owed at least as much, in its early stages, to monks from Ireland and Scotland as to official missionaries sent from Rome; and that for a considerable period of its early history the English Church had only distant and intermittent relations with Rome. But with the Norman Conquest, England was brought into the full orbit of European civilization and culture; and therefore into closer relations with the papacy, at that time directed by one of the ablest of popes, Hildebrand or Gregory VII. The natural result of this association was seen in a revival of religious life and zeal, in better ecclesiastical organization, in the building of some of our most famous cathedrals, and in the strengthening of the power and independence of the Church over against the State. Upon occasion this might find expression in conflicts between kings and archbishops, as between Henry I and Archbishop Anselm, or, most famous of all, between Henry II and Becket; but the reliance of these archbishops on the backing of the papacy greatly strengthened their hand against the monarchs. Indeed so submissive was England to the policy of Rome during the long reign of Henry III, which spanned more than half of the thirteenth century, that it became known as the milch-cow of the papacy. During this century, moreover, the learning, zeal, and organization of the western Church attained its greatest heights; and nowhere was its influence more fully and beneficently felt than in this country. Nor was the benefit altogether one-sided. If Italians such as Lanfranc and Anselm became Archbishops of Canterbury, Englishmen might become bishops in foreign countries, as Gilbert of Hastings became first Bishop of Lisbon, and one of our countrymen, Nicolas Breakspear even ascended the papal chair as Adrian IV.

Such a close relationship could not persist throughout several centuries without occasions of friction. For the papacy, like all forms of government, had to be supported financially; and those who benefited from the administrative system centred in the Roman curia, or enjoyed the judicial procedure based on the Roman Canon Law, had to pay for the privilege of being so governed. The only means of maintaining this expensive administrative and legal machinery was by taxation; whether in the form of taxes levied on individuals, such as the first-fruits and tenths of ecclesiastical benefices, or Peter's Pence collected from the laity; or in the form of what were called papal provisions; that is, the appointment by the papacy to benefices in England of clerics employed in the Roman curia; who were not expected, of course, to leave their duties there and reside upon these distant cures. Englishmen are traditionally famous for their grumbling about taxation; and medieval Englishmen grumbled about paying taxes to Rome as their modern descendants do about Budget day in the present century. Similarly, some anticipations of later patriotic and insular rebellions were aroused when the papacy interfered directly in appointments to the highest offices in the English Church. For example, the beginning of the long quarrel between King John and the papacy, which led to his surrender of his kingdom to the pope and his receiving it again as a papal fief, lay in a dispute between king and pope about the filling of the archbishopric of Canterbury. Thrice indeed during the thirteenth century, when the medieval papacy was at the height of its prestige, did Rome force its own nominee into the see of Canterbury, overriding English influence. But when Shakespeare puts into the mouth of his *King John* these words of defiance to the pope:

> *Tell him this tale, and from the mouth of England*
> *Add thus much more, that no Italian priest*
> *Shall tithe or toll in our dominions;*
> *But as we, under heaven, are supreme head*
> *So under Him that great supremacy,*
> *Where we do reign, we will alone uphold.*

he is speaking with the accents of Elizabethan not of medieval England. The hands are those of John, but the voice is that of Henry VIII.

What sharpened national animosity in England against Rome was the political consequence of Anglo-French rivalry and of tortuous papal diplomacy. When the Hundred Years' War brought England and France into mortal conflict, there arose a demand for the prevention of revenues of English religious houses from being sent abroad to an enemy country. Therefore some alien priories were suppressed and their income confiscated. At the same time there occurred in 1305 the episode in papal history known at the Babylonish Captivity at Avignon, whereby a succession of popes ceased to live in Rome and withdrew to the city on the Rhône. This increased the English suspicion, albeit unjust, that the papacy was becoming an ally of the national enemy; and led to further demands for reprisals against Rome. Acts of Parliament, known as the Statutes of Provisors and Praemunire were therefore passed, to prevent the popes from providing foreign clerics to English benefices. Even worse was to follow for the papacy in 1378, when the Great Schism presented Christendom with the spectacle of rival popes, each claiming to be the true holder of the office and excommunicating his rival. Thus the various states of Europe openly took sides with one or other of the rivals, from purely political motives.

When, therefore, the Earl of Warwick and the Bishop of Beauvais met in the former's tent outside Rouen in the first quarter of the fifteenth century, nationalism was coming to the surface as a force of novel and unknown potentiality, particularly in the kingdoms of France and England. Beyond doubt it was one of the twin factors which were to bring about the sixteenth century Reformation; and nowhere more obviously so than in England. But to do this, it was necessary that it should be reinforced by a more properly religious element; which was to be supplied by that 'Protestantism', which the English nobleman claimed already to discern as its handmaid and ally.

2. THE HERITAGE OF THE MIDDLE AGES

(ii) 'PROTESTANTISM'

To Peter Cauchon, Bishop of Beauvais, in his conversation with the Earl of Warwick in Bernard Shaw's *St. Joan*, the chief portent about Joan of Arc was that 'she has never once mentioned the Church, and thinks only of God and herself'. When the English nobleman identified this attitude as 'Protestantism', the French prelate replied: 'You understand it wonderfully well, my lord. Scratch an Englishman and find a Protestant.' The history of English religion since the Reformation has done much to confirm the popular impression that an Englishman is an inveterate Protestant. But it is perhaps of greater importance to observe how near the playwright has come to the heart of Protestantism in his definition of it as 'the protest of the individual soul against the interference of the priest between the private man and his God'. More than four centuries later indeed, John Henry Newman, one of the greatest ornaments in the nineteenth century first of the Church of England and then of that of Rome, in describing the effect of his Evangelical conversion, wrote that it had made him conscious of 'two and two only supreme, luminously self-evident beings, myself and my Creator'.

But if the essence of Protestantism consists in its insistence on the immediate and direct relationship of the individual soul and God, then it is obvious that the emergence of such a high degree of individual self-consciousness was a late development of the middle ages. For medieval society was essentially corporate; and men were envisaged less as individual personalities than as members of groups, whether of the Church, or the University, or the Gild. In some respects indeed medieval society was more akin to the corporative and totalitarian states of the present age than to nineteenth century patterns of society. One of the earliest forerunners of change was John Wyclif, an Oxford scholar and teacher in the fourteenth century. In older text-books of history he was described as 'the morning-star of the Reformation'; but deeper study has shown that he was, as could only be expected, a man of his age, though some of his principles led ultimately if indirectly to the Reformation. He began as a critic of practical abuses in the Church; and only when he found these well defended by vested interests, did he turn to examine the theology on which they rested. He became famous for his denial and refutation of the doctrine of transubstantiation; though here also he argued, not as a 'Protestant', but as the champion of one school of scholastic philosophy, the realist, against the other, the nominalist. Later thinkers were to carry this denial to much further lengths. More important perhaps was his individualism. Religion for him had the purpose of saving those particular souls whom God wills to be saved; and the Church therefore is only a means to this end, not an end in itself. He repudiated the necessity of the papacy to the visible Church; and held that bishop and priest were but one and the same order of ministry. But his greatest practical achievement was the first translation of the Bible into English. In accordance with his conviction that the Bible is the Law of God and the authority for Christian belief, he desired that its text should be available in English. From this it followed that the reading and preaching of the Bible became a primary duty and privilege for his followers; and when the official Church, in the person of Archbishop Arundel, sought to stamp out these new tendencies by limiting preaching to persons specially licensed, and by discouraging these practices generally, it merely drove underground the movement known as Lollardy.

It would be difficult to overestimate the far-reaching importance of Wyclif's translation of the Bible into English; and the inspiration and impetus which it gave to the reading and preaching of the Word of God. Evidences of this crop up in many and various, and sometimes perhaps surprising, places. Thus, for example, John Whitgift, the third of Queen Elizabeth I's Archbishops of Canterbury, remembered his own education as a boy in the Augustinian house at Wellow, near Grimsby, under the tutelage of his uncle, Robert, the abbot; and he recollected particularly some words of Robert 'that he had read the Holy Scriptures over and over but could never find there that their religion was founded of God'; so that he foretold its early overthrow. Again, there is evidence that Wyclif's successors, generally called the 'known men', or the 'just, fast men', supplied a continuous and unbroken link between medieval Lollardy and sixteenth-century Lutheranism in England. For these *colporteurs* of the Scriptures, carrying single books of the Bible where copies of the whole could not be had, from place to place, and encouraging little groups to meet secretly for their reading and exposition, ensured that Wyclif's influence did not perish. John Foxe, the industrious Protestant martyrologist, called them and their disciples 'the secret multitude of true professors'. Whether they were in fact a multitude may be uncertain; but they were certainly secret; and they did their work so well that when Lutheranism reached England in the reign of Henry VIII it seemed at first sight but a continuation of Lollardy.

Of only slightly less importance from a popular and practical standpoint were the results of Wyclif's denial of transubstantiation; which carried grave consequences for the medieval system of religion and for the priesthood. For medieval catholicism was centred in the Mass, which the layman was expected to attend on Sundays and Holy days, and at which he made his annual communion at Easter. But the Mass was also a sacrifice, offered for the living and the departed; and a prominent feature of later medieval religion was the extraordinary growth of Obits, or Masses for the departed. Thus Henry V provided by will for the saying of 20,000 Masses for the repose of his soul; and Henry VI for 10,000 to be said within one month of his death. Lower in the social scale came such persons as the father of Dean Colet, a Lord Mayor of London, who ordered two priests to say Mass daily for his soul for fifteen years; or the Lady Alice West who ordered the saying within a fortnight of her death of 4,400 Masses at the rate of only one penny per Mass. From these practices there sprang a kind of arithmetical evaluation of the efficacy of Masses, and a widespread popular revulsion against the Mass itself, combined with a low estimation of the priesthood ordained to discharge these offices. When this popular aversion was combined with Lollard denials of transubstantiation, the way was prepared for such sixteeenth century explosions of blasphemy as those which referred to the consecrated Host as 'Jack in the Box', or 'Round Robin' or 'Hocus Pocus'. In more respects than one the seeds of Protestantism were germinating in the later middle ages.

Other factors lent their aid. The widespread mystical movement of the late fourteenth and fifteenth centuries, significantly known as the *Devotio Moderna*, introduced the educated circles which it penetrated to religious exercises, which were designed to cultivate direct and immediate relationship of the individual soul and God. Such personal religious experience may easily become subjective, and impatient of the objective standards and restraints of the Church. Moreover, all these tendencies both expressed and accentuated the individualism which was to become a prominent feature of the modern world, alike in religious and secular activities. When the invention of printing enabled the rapid multiplication of translations of the Bible into the vernacular, Protestantism was standing on the threshold, waiting for the lifting of the latch. The old order of the middle ages was breaking up, in politics, in religion, and in thought. The peculiar circumstances of England under its new national monarchy of the Tudor dynasty, fused the twin forces of Nationalism and Protestantism, to produce the particular characteristics of the English Reformation.

3. THE ENGLISH REFORMATION

(i) Constitutional

In my first two talks, I said something about two great forces, Nationalism and Protestantism, both springing out of the medieval order, but working to undermine its characteristic institutions. In my next two talks, I shall try to show how these forces brought about the English Reformation of the sixteenth century; and in so doing, marked the beginning of the distinctively English contribution to religious life and thought, and to the development of Church, State, and Society in England.

The element of Nationalism is plainly stamped upon the face of the English Reformation. In the preamble to one of the most important statutes of the Reformation Parliament of Henry VIII, the Act of Appeals, one of the fundamental principles of the English Reformation was vigorously, if quaintly, expressed. 'By divers, sundry, old authentic histories and chronicles, it is manifestly declared and expressed that this realm of England is an empire, and so hath been accepted in the world, governed by one supreme head and king'. Here was a blunt assertion of the national unity and sovereignty of England, as independent of the jurisdiction of the Holy Roman papacy in religion as of the corresponding authority in the secular sphere of the Holy Roman emperor. It was the canonization, as it were, of the principle of nationalism applied to religion. Therefore it is hardly an exaggeration to say that on its constitutional side, the Reformation in England amounted to the substitution of the royal supremacy for the papal headship of the Church. By the Act of Supremacy indeed the king was to 'be taken, accepted and reputed the only supreme head in earth of the Church of England'. Under the similar Act of Supremacy passed at the beginning of Elizabeth I's reign, the royal title was modified and softened to 'Supreme Governor'; but the effect was little different. Henceforth the Church of England was to be subjected to the Crown as its supreme authority in legislative, administrative, and judicial matters; and the papacy was thrown out of doors.

Essentially there was nothing revolutionary in this assertion of the rights of the king. Marsilius of Padua in 1324 had laid down its principles in his *Defensor Pacis*. In sixteenth century Spain, the sovereigns Ferdinand and Isabella forced through an administrative and financial reform of the Church in the teeth of papal opposition; and in the next century in France Louis XIV, by his assertion of the famous Gallican Liberties and by his own practice, claimed extensive powers for the French crown over the Church. In the eighteenth century too, Joseph II of Austria used his imperial authority to compel reforms, despite the opposition of Rome. All these rulers stopped short indeed of a complete and entire repudiation of the papacy; but when, during the first quarter of the eighteenth century, a correspondence was begun between Archbishop Wake of Canterbury and two theologians of the Sorbonne, to explore the possibilities of an union between the Churches of England and France, the English primate pointed out how nearly France under Louis XIV had come to the Anglican position in regard to the royal supremacy.

It should not be supposed however that the royal supremacy was a mere political *ruse de guerre*. Sixteenth century reformers made it a point of pride to base their work on the authority of the Bible; and nowhere was this more the case than with the powers which they ascribed to the king. In the words of Article XXXVII of the Thirty-Nine Articles of Religion (which in the reign of Elizabeth I became the official statement of Anglican doctrine): 'We give not to our princes the ministering either of God's Word or of the Sacraments; but that only prerogative which we see to have been given always to all godly Princes in Holy Scriptures by God himself; that is, that they should rule all estates and degrees committed to their charge by God, whether they be Ecclesiastical or Temporal'. In the Old Testament historical books, the reformers saw a pattern of government, which, as they believed, was divinely ordained by God for His chosen people the Hebrews, during the period of their national independence. There in the kingship of the Old Covenant, the sovereign was superior to the priesthood, was charged with the responsibility for the religion no less than the politics of his state, and was over all persons and in all causes supreme. How much more then must this be true when the godly Prince was a Christian monarch? Not only Lutheran princes on the continent, nor bishops of Protestant leanings in England such as Cranmer, but prelates of Catholic orthodoxy like Stephen Gardiner, agreed in this exaltation of the authority of the crown in matters of religion. Richard Hooker summed up the Anglican position in these words: 'Our state is according to the pattern of God's own, ancient, elect people; which people was not part of them the commonwealth, and part of them the church of God; but the self-same people, whole and entire, were both under one chief Governor, on whose authority they did all depend.' In some Lutheran states of Germany indeed the godly Prince claimed higher titles; and the King of Prussia, until the establishment of the German Empire in 1871, retained the title of *summus episcopus*, or chief bishop. But though the English Reformation claimed for the sovereign only a power of jurisdiction over the Church and clergy, not a power of Order, the royal supremacy was the corner-stone of that Reformation; and gave to the king wide powers in ecclesiastical matters. Over against the authority claimed by the Pope, for which the reformers alleged that there was no warrant in the Bible, was set the power of the godly Prince, firmly buttressed by appeals to the Old and New Testaments.

This royal supremacy could find expression in many and various ways. It might be exercised through Convocation, which, subject to the king's licence and authorization, could make Canons for the government of the Church, as was done notably under James I in 1603. Or the king migh proceed by Act of Parliament, as was the case with all the reforming measures of Henry VIII; and also, during the reigns of Edward VI and Elizabeth I, successive English Prayer Books were authorized by Acts of Uniformity. Again, the sovereign could act by Royal Injunctions, addressed by Henry VIII, Edward VI, and Elizabeth I to the archbishops and bishops for enforcement in their dioceses. Thus the long arm of the crown made itself felt throughout all branches of the administration of the Church of England; especially when Elizabeth I set up for the better exercise of her judicial power, a Court of High Commission to deal with ecclesiastical suits. This system worked well enough so long as there was no sharp difference of religious policy between the sovereign and parliament on the one hand, nor clash of religious allegiance between the sovereign and the Church on the other. Under the Tudor dynasty, the royal supremacy was an advantage and asset to the Church; but under James I and Charles I the chasm between Crown and House of Commons in religious policy became wider and deeper; so that the Church fell with the monarchy, in the civil war of the seventeenth century. Later, when the Stuart house had been restored to the throne, the secret profession of Roman Catholicism by Charles II and its open championship by James II led to a decisive clash between Crown and Church; so that in 1688 James II fled the country; and the Dutch Calvinist Prince, William of Orange, was called to the throne. The royal supremacy therefore might be either a defence and protection, or a handicap and obstacle, to the Church; but it was a factor of the utmost importance during the stormy two hundred years between the accession of Henry VIII and that of the House of Hanover.

4. THE ENGLISH REFORMATION

(ii) The Prayer Books

During the reign of Henry VIII, the Reformation amounted to little more than Catholicism without the pope. Henry indeed boasted of his unswerving orthodoxy of belief. The Act in Restraint of Annates declared that his subjects were 'as devout, obedient, catholic and humble children of God and holy Church as any people be within any realm christened'. Similarly, the Act stopping Peter's Pence insisted that there was no intention 'to decline or vary from the congregation of Christ's Church in any things concerning the very articles of the Catholic Faith of Christendom, or in any other things declared by Holy Scripture and the Word of God, necessary for your and their salvation'. So long as Henry reigned therefore, the movement for Protestant reform in liturgy and belief was driven underground to a large extent. None the less, it was present and germinating. Henry's own Archbishop of Canterbury, Thomas Cranmer, had been influenced by Lutheran doctrines, both as a student at Cambridge and during diplomatic journeys in Germany. Lutheran books and pamphlets were smuggled into England; and if Cranmer's approaches in the direction of Protestant doctrine were tentative and modest during Henry's lifetime, he was preparing for times of greater freedom.

With the accession of the young King Edward VI, who had been taught to consider himself cast for the part of King Josiah in the English Reformation, the floodgates of change were opened. In 1549 there appeared the first Prayer Book in English, with a complete body of services for Morning and Evening prayer, for the Holy Communion, and for the occasional Offices of Baptism, Confirmation, Marriage, and Burial. On the whole it was a conservative work. It contained elements from Eastern and Lutheran liturgies; but chiefly it was based upon the medieval English Rite of Sarum. The central rite of the Communion retained the traditional title of the Mass; and was cast also in traditional mould. Bishop Stephen Gardiner found it patient of a Catholic interpretation, as implying, though not explicitly affirming, the doctrine of transubstantiation; and the medieval Mass vestments were to be worn at its celebration. Its principal innovations were the use of the English vernacular throughout (even for the most sacred part of the Canon, namely the words of consecration of the elements); and the communicating of the people in both species, giving them the cup as well as the bread. The office for the Baptism of infants retained exorcism and the vesting of the child in the chrisom; and that of Confirmation required the bishop to cross the children in the forehead as well as to lay his hands upon them. But the very circumstance that orthodox bishops like Gardiner could find this English Communion patient of interpretation in terms of transubstantiation, made it obnoxious to advanced reformers, particularly to those foreign divines like Martin Bucer, who had been invited to this country as professors of divinity. It seems probable indeed that Cranmer himself thought of the 1549 Prayer Book only as an interim measure and a first instalment of reform, to last until his own more radical standpoint had found expression in a further Rite, and designed to wean the people by degrees from the old order.

Accordingly in 1552 there appeared the Second Prayer Book of Edward VI; in which signs of advanced Protestant doctrine and of Calvinist influence were plainly evident. The permissive title of 'The Mass' disappeared; the Communion Service was radically reconstructed to remove all the points urged by Gardiner in favour of a Catholic interpretation and to meet the criticism of Bucer; the words of administration of the elements to the communicants stressed the purely commemorative aspect of the rite; and the wearing of the traditional vestments was expressly forbidden, the use of the surplice only being required. It is difficult to interpret this Communion service as implying other than a commemorative view of the Eucharist and a receptionist doctrine of the presence of Christ's body and blood. Cranmer had crossed the Rubicon, by the removal of the ambiguities of the first Prayer Book which had allowed a Catholic interpretation. It is important therefore to observe that when, after the reaction under Mary Tudor, Elizabeth I restored the royal supremacy, the Prayer Book authorized by her Act of Uniformity of 1559 was substantially the Second Prayer Book of 1552. Two significant changes indeed were made. At the communion of the people the words of administration of the 1549 Prayer Book were joined with those of 1552; so as to read, 'The body (or blood) of our Lord Jesus Christ . . . preserve thy body and soul unto everlasting life; take and eat (or drink) this, in remembrance that Christ died for thee (or that Christ's blood was shed for thee).' The purpose of this change was plain; to allow belief in the presence of Christ not only in the heart of the faithful recipient, but also in the elements themselves. The second change ordered the wearing of the medieval vestments; so that the new Communion service might look like the old in externals. It seems very probable indeed that the Queen herself would have preferred the 1549 Prayer Book; but that the strong Puritan element in the House of Commons in 1559 compelled the adoption of the 1552 Book.

Perhaps of equal importance were the changes taking place in the interior appearance of the parish churches. Henry VIII's reign had seen the beginning of a purging of the churches of images which might be the object of superstitious reverence; and that of Elizabeth I completed the process. Henceforth the parish church walls were whitewashed, thus obliterating medieval mural paintings; the east wall had the Lord's Prayer, the Apostles' Creed, the Ten Commandments, and some sentences of Scripture painted upon it; and beneath stood a simple Table in the place of the destroyed stone altar. Even the requirement about the wearing of the old vestments could not be enforced because of the general holocaust of such ornaments of the church and of the ministers thereof. The English parish churches to the outward eye seemed much more akin to the Calvinist churches of the continent than to those of the Lutheran Reformation.

The chief and most influential of all Henry VIII's reforms, however, had been his order in the Royal Injunctions of 1538, for the setting up in every parish church of 'one book of the whole Bible of the largest volume in English'; not only for the clergy but also for the people to read. It would be difficult to overestimate the importance of this step in the long-distance development of English religion. Not only did the Bible become the standard of doctrine in the Church, but also the book of private devotion and piety of the people. Together with the Book of Common Prayer, it moulded the public worship of the Church; and it became the pattern and inspiration of individual religion. When, in 1563, the Church of England defined its doctrinal position in relation to contemporary controversies, in the Thirty-Nine Articles of Religion, the work of religious reformation was complete in essentials. A threefold cord is not quickly broken; and in the Prayer Book, Bible, and Articles of Religion, the Church of England's position was set forth, as representing a *via media* between Rome and Geneva. At first, perhaps, this was little more than an aspiration; but the storms and conflicts of a century were to turn it into a reality.

5. THE ELIZABETHAN SETTLEMENT

'By the goodness of almighty God, and his servant Elizabeth, we are.' In these words Richard Hooker gave expression to his grateful sense of the protection accorded to the Church of England against its adversaries by Elizabeth I. At first sight his eulogy may seem exaggerated; and the historian would place sundry items to the debit as well as to the credit side of the queen's account. But substantially it reflected the conviction of contemporary churchmen that under her rule, the royal supremacy had not only been a defence and protection, but had saved the religious settlement from extinction. Let us look a little more closely into the circumstances of her long and vitally important reign.

One of the chief characteristics of the Anglican Reformation, which has not been mentioned hitherto, was the retention of the three-fold Order of Ministry, comprising Bishops, Priests, and Deacons. This order, together with the provision of forms for admitting men to the several grades, had been laid down during the reign of Edward VI by the authorization of the Ordinal; first issued in 1550, and then revised and reissued as part of the Prayer Book of 1552. Admission to each grade of the ministry was by imposition of hands with prayer; and by the handing to the candidate of part or the whole of the Bible; the deacon receiving the New Testament, and the priest or bishop the whole Bible. But Elizabeth I at her accession was faced by the acute difficulty that of the surviving Marian bishops all save one refused to take the new oath to herself as Supreme Governor, and he the octogenarian bishop of Llandaff. The utmost care was therefore taken in all the rite for the consecration of her new primate, Matthew Parker, to the archbishopric of Canterbury; and rivers of ink have been spilled in minute and controversial examination of this crucial episode. It is possible therefore only to state one's own conclusions without the detailed evidence on which they rest. Matthew Parker was consecrated in the chapel of Lambeth Palace on Sunday, December 17th, 1559, according to the English Ordinal, by Bishop Barlow and Bishop Scory, both of whom had been deprived of their sees under Mary and were now only bishops-elect of other dioceses; assisted by Bishop Coverdale, an Edwardian diocesan bishop now without office, and the Bishop-suffragan of Bedford, John Hodgkin. Of these, Barlow and Hodgkin had been consecrated during Henry VIII's reign; and since the record of Barlow's consecration is missing from Cranmer's Register (like that of other contemporary bishops), desperate efforts have been made to show that he was never consecrated. It must suffice to say that these are too improbable to carry conviction; and that so far as Barlow and the English Ordinal went, Matthew Parker was duly and truly consecrated Archbishop of Canterbury.

But this was only the beginning of troubles. Thanks to the defection of the Marian bishops, Elizabeth had to replenish the episcopate chiefly from the number of those divines who, during the Marian persecution, had fled abroad to the continent for refuge. There they had seen the Calvinist reformed churches in full splendour; and had blushed for the compromises even of the 1552 English Prayer Book. Accordingly there began a long struggle for the enforcement of the minimum of rites and ceremonies in the Elizabethan Church. Soon it became obvious that the wearing of the medieval vestments could not be enforced; and Parker fell back on the cope. This too could not be enforced; and by 1566 he had to try and compel the wearing of the surplice only at the celebration of the Communion. Even so, the first Nonconformity emerged as a protest against the surplice; and at the same time, the more radical clergy took the law into their own hands, by omitting such parts of the Book of Common Prayer as were obnoxious to them. Parker struggled bravely, but with only moderate success, to secure a minimum standard of uniformity; whilst his successor at Canterbury, Edmund Grindal, was too much in sympathy with the Puritans to take drastic action, and was suspended by the queen for his refusal so to do. Not until John Whitgift became primate and was supported by the Court of High Commission, a prerogative court in authority and procedure, was the heavy hand of coercion brought into play to enforce outward conformity.

For the truth of the matter was that the Elizabethan settlement was under fire from two opposite standpoints. On the one hand were the Roman Catholic recusants, who, in obedience to the papal bull of 1570 excommunicating Elizabeth, withdrew from the established Church; and on the other were the advanced Puritans, who wished to overthow the compromises of 1559 and to advance to the full Genevan pattern. From the standpoint of the Church of England, these controversies gave birth to two classic defences of its position and teaching. Against the recusants, John Jewel, Bishop of Salisbury, published in 1562 his *Apologie or Answere in defence of the Church of England*. In it he pointed to the retention by his Church of the three creeds, the threefold order of ministry, and the two sacraments of the Gospel, as evidence that it had 'returned to the apostles and old catholic fathers'. At the same time he specified the corruptions and errors of Rome which had been rejected, challenged his opponents to establish their case from the Scriptures and the early Fathers; and defended the royal against the papal supremacy. 'It is true,' he wrote, 'we have departed from them. . . . But yet for all this, from the primitive Church, from the apostles, and from Christ we have not departed'; and his conclusion was that 'we have forsaken the Church as it is now, not as it was in old times past'.

The more aggressive and dangerous attack, however, was from the Puritan side, whence came the campaign for 'the reform of the reformation', the removal of everything deriving from the old order, and the demand for specific Biblical authority for all things done in the Church. The defence of the established Church against this radical assault fell to the lot of the greatest scholar of the Elizabethan Church, and one of the greatest ornaments of Anglicanism in all centuries, Richard Hooker, Master of the Temple. In his massive apologia *Of the Laws of Ecclesiastical Polity*, he laid the foundations of the justification of the Anglican *via media*. His work opened with a majestic examination of the scope of law in the universe, medieval in concept and character, by which he refuted the Puritan claim that the Bible only contains the law of God. He appealed to a triple authority in his exegesis of the Anglican position, to Scripture, Tradition, and Reason. Of these, Scripture, of course, was pre-eminent; and where it spoke with an unequivocal voice, and particularly in all things necessary to be believed for salvation, its authority was paramount. But in matters where the testimony of Scripture was less than certain, it was wise to consult the tradition of the Church; as, for example, in the retention of episcopacy by the Church of England. Moreover, Hooker recognized human reason as a gift of God, and likewise to be consulted in the determination of things indifferent in their own nature. Thus he could not allow the Puritan contention that specific Biblical precept must be required for everything done in the worship, polity, and ceremonies of the Church. His *apologia* was at once comprehensive, charitable, and catholic. Perhaps its greatest effect was to give self-confidence to the Anglicans of his generation, reminding them that, 'We had rather glorify and bless God for the fruit we daily behold reaped by such ordinances as

His gracious Spirit maketh the ripe wisdom of this national Church to bring forth . . . we make not our childish appeals sometimes from our own to foreign churches, sometimes from both unto churches ancienter than both are, in effect always from all others to our own selves, but as becometh them that follow with all humility the ways of peace, we honour, reverence, and obey in the very next degree unto God, the voice of the church of God wherein we live.'

6. ELIZABETHAN PURITANISM

(i) Presbyterianism

'Marry, sir, sometimes he is a kind of Puritan,' observed Maria of Malvolio in Shakespeare's *Twelfth Night*. To which Sir Andrew Aguecheek replied: 'O, if I thought that, I'd beat him like a dog'; and, when challenged by his companion, Sir Toby Belch: 'What, for being a Puritan? Thy exquisite reason, dear knight?' could only answer: 'I have no exquisite reason for't, but I have reason good enough.' It may have been natural that the name of Puritan should provoke these gentlemen in their cups; but the playwright's introduction of the name, and the character given by Ben Jonson to his *Zeal-of-the-Land-Busy,* indicate more than a little contemporary dislike of Puritanism. Yet the movement thus caricatured was one of the most important religious influences in Elizabethan England; and its essential conviction was that the Church of England represented but an uneasy half-way house between Rome and Geneva, and needed 'the reform of the reformation' to make it complete and self-consistent.

The first sign of this temper was manifest at the very beginning of the reign. For it has been established that the strong Puritan element in the House of Commons of Elizabeth's first parliament in 1559, obtained its will against the queen by insisting that the Act of Supremacy should be accompanied by an Act of Uniformity; and that the Prayer Book thus authorized should be the Second, not the First, of Edward VI's books. From the outset, however, many of the clergy and laity were dissatisfied with this service-book. The conflict began about the wearing of the surplice; and in 1567 Archbishop Parker had to deprive several of the ablest and leading London clergy for nonconformity in this respect. Out of his action there sprang the first nonconforming congregation, which met at Plumbers' Hall and used John Knox's Genevan Service Book. Soon the controversy centred in more important and vital issues, namely a demand for the replacement of episcopacy by the Presbyterian order of church government, and of the Book of Common Prayer by Calvin's order of public worship. This Puritan movement of the age of Elizabeth I might without injustice be called the Cambridge Movement; for its principal leaders, both in its Presbyterian and Independent forms, came from that university. The first blast of the Presbyterian trumpet indeed was sounded by Thomas Cartwright, Lady Margaret Professor of Divinity, in his lectures on the Acts of the Apostles; in which he demanded the remodelling of the polity of the Church of England in accordance with that of the primitive Church.

From the university the agitation spread to the forum; and found mordant expression in 1572 in a first *Admonition to Parliament*, the equivalent of our modern 'Open Letter to a Member of Parliament'. 'May it therefore please your wysedoms to understand,' the authors of this manifesto wrote: 'We in England are so fare of, from having a church rightly reformed accordying to the prescripte of Gods worde, that as yet we are not come to the outwarde face of the same. . . . The outwarde markes wherby a true christian church is knowne, are preaching of the worde purely, ministering of the sacraments sincerely, and ecclesiastical discipline which consisteth in admonition and correction of faults severelie.' On all three counts the established church was deemed insufficient. Its ministry was neither rightly appointed nor educated; its sacraments were still hedged about with 'synging, pypyng, surplesse and cope wearing'; whilst it was a byword amongst reformed Churches for its lack of a proper discipline of the laity. Further, the writers could not withhold censure of the Prayer Book; calling it 'an unperfecte booke, culled and picked out of that popishe dunghill, the Masse booke, full of all abhominations'. Later in the same year a *Seconde Admonition* supplied what was lacking in the first, by setting forth the remedies. The ministry should consist of pastors, teachers, elders, and deacons; and rules for the method of their appointment were laid down, with a description of their respective duties. The pastors should meet in local conferences, to 'exercise themselves in prophesying or interpreting the scriptures'; and there should be provincial and national synods. Each congregation must have a consistory, composed of the pastor and chosen lay elders, to administer discipline over the people; and the final penalty should be excommunication; which 'is a fearfull thing, as it is prescribed by the scriptures, and used by the Churches of Christ reformed accordingly. No punishment to it in this worlde, but only hell eternally.'

The purpose of these manifestos was to induce parliament to remodel the church settlement. For the Presbyterian believed firmly in a national, established church; and if queen and bishops would not respond, then parliament should; for it had enacted the Acts of Uniformity and Supremacy; and what it had fashioned, it could refashion. The name generally given by contemporaries to this programme was that of 'tarrying for the magistrate'; that is, seeking reform by constitutional means. It failed because Elizabeth I would not allow the House of Commons to meddle with her church settlement; and, faced with this dilemma, what could the Presbyterians do next? They had begun already to institute the famous exercises known as 'prophesyings'; which consisted of meetings of local ministers, to which laymen were sometimes admitted, at which passages of scriptures were expounded. These exercises were of undoubted value in raising the standard of clerical education, which was deplorably low; and many bishops, including Archbishop Grindal, wished to regulate them. The queen, however, insisted on their suppression.

Next, therefore, the Presbyterians embarked upon a bolder move. They began to introduce their ecclesiastical system, upon a purely voluntary and consensual basis, within the framework of the establishment. This movement, known as the *Classis*, was particularly strong in East Anglia and the Midlands. Ministers in sympathy with Presbyterianism submitted to episcopal ordination and to the method of private patronage, but at the same time offered themselves for approval and election by the congregation before accepting a benefice; and preferred to call themselves pastors rather than vicars or rectors. They met together in local gatherings for mutual exhortation and reproof; and such of the laity as were willing to subject themselves to ecclesiastical discipline, followed suit. Correspondence was maintained between various of these gatherings, and something approaching a common policy was reached; especially when petitions were sent to parliament. At a meeting in London of several local Classes in 1583, it was agreed that 'they might proceed thus far, and keep notwithstanding the peace of the Church of England established'. In the same year, when John Whitgift became Archbishop of Canterbury, the *Classis* at Dedham in Essex decided 'that it were good the archbishop should be written unto, to be favourable to the Church and to discipline'. But soon word came from London that Whitgift, 'now he is in, sheweth himself as he was wont to be. . . . The peace of the church is at an end if he be not curbed.'

It was the Presbyterians, however, and not the primate, who were to be curbed. With the backing of the queen and by means of the reconstituted Court of High Commission, severe measures were taken against all nonconformists; and Cartwright himself was brought to imprisonment and trial. To a considerable extent the Presbyterian movement was driven underground; and its tarrying for the magistrate was to continue for more than half a century longer, until during the civil wars of the seventeenth century, it enjoyed a short and fleeting triumph. It should be observed that its system was not one of church democracy. Though the pastor was elected by the people and administered discipline with the help of lay elders chosen by the congregation, the presbyters claimed all the powers exercised by the New Testament presbyter or bishop. They were a permanent order of ministry, entrusted with authority to preach, teach, administer the sacraments and execute ecclesiastical censures. For more than a century and a half, Presbyterianism was the strongest and largest body of Protestant dissent. But already it was being challenged by a more extreme and more democratic version of Puritanism, which repudiated alike its constitutional moderation and its tarrying for the magistrate. This new radical movement adopted the maxim of 'reformation without tarrying for anie'; and it is of this movement, the parent of Independency and of the Baptist churches, that I shall next speak.

7. ELIZABETHAN PURITANISM

(ii) Independents and Baptists

'I HAD as lief be a Brownist as a politician,' observed Sir Andrew Aguecheek in one of his pleasantries in Shakespeare's *Twelfth Night*; and in neither case was the reference intended to be complimentary. For the Brownists were those radical Puritans who differed from the Presbyterians of whom I spoke last week, by their refusal to stay and work for reform within the established Church. They took as their maxim and principle of action the title of a pamphlet written by Robert Browne, *A Treatise of Reformation without tarrying for anie*, and they put into action their convictions by forming Separatist churches outside the national Church. They are of the utmost importance therefore in the history of religious and political thought in England, as the first dissenters who defied the combined authority of Church and State on the ground of conscience and duty to God.

The beginnings of Separatism indeed may be traced to 1567, when a congregation gathered in London under Richard Fitz, the members of which bound themselves to Christ and to each other by a Covenant, not to return to 'these reliques of Antichriste' and to 'them that have receaved these markes of the Romysh beast' in the Church of England. Such 'privye churches' were naturally fugitive and evanescent; and the Separatist movement received its next powerful impetus from Robert Browne and Robert Harrison, two Cambridge men, who in 1582 fled to Middleburgh in the United Provinces to escape persecution. There Browne adumbrated the principles of Independency. Particularly he enunciated with clarity and force the maxim of a 'gathered' church. 'The Church planted or gathered is a company or number of Christians or believers, which, by a willing Covenant made with their God, are under the government of God and Christ, and keep his laws in one holy communion.' Browne had no use for the mixed multitude of nominal Christians whom both the establishment and the Presbyterians would have included in their membership. For him the church consisted only of those whom God had called out of the midst of a naughty world to be His elect. In such a church the civil magistrate could have neither power nor authority; much less could any profit come from tarrying for the magistrate to effect the reformation. That must begin with 'the worthiest, were they never so few', in every parish. The authority of Christ moreover was exercised, not by a clerical hierarchy, whether episcoal or presbyterian, but by the holy people of God in the local congregation. Thus Browne laid down the principles of Congregationalist church polity; though he subsequently conformed to and was beneficed in the established Church.

But if he failed to rise to the height of his vocation as a confessor, Henry Barrowe, John Greenwood, and John Penry were to become martyrs for Independency. Barrowe, particularly, developed the essentially democratic character of its church government. He based his doctrine on Scripture and the illumination of the Holy Spirit; and he affirmed that all church members were 'ecclesiastical and spiritual'; for, he added, 'we know not what you mean by your old popish terms of laymen'. The local church in all its members therefore made 'one body unto Christ; all the affairs of the church belong to that body together'. There was indeed a differentiation of function and office, but not of order. Appointment to all offices in the church, whether pastor, teacher, elder, or deacon, was 'by the holy and free election of the Lord's holy people; and that according to the Lord's ordinance; humbling themselves by fasting and prayer, craving the direction of His Holy Spirit for the trial and approving of their gifts'. By this means 'hath everyone of the people interest in the election and ordination of their officers'. The flock was therefore anterior to the pastor; and conceivably a congregation, by 'no default or negligence in them', might continue for some time having 'as yet attained to have neither a ministry nor sacraments'; for in Barrowe's view, even sacraments 'are not a perpetual mark of the church'. By insisting on liberty for any member of the church to prophesy if the Lord gave him utterance, Barrowe emphasized still further the democratic nature of his church polity. 'The least member of the church that is a communicant, hath as much interest in all the censures of the church as the pastor, and have equal power according to the rules of the Word to censure the pastor for error or transgression, as the pastor hath to censure them.' Thus was realized the model of a Christian democracy, which in due season would spread from the ordering of a church to that of a commonwealth. Moreover, although the martyrdoms of Barrowe, Greenwood, and Penry led to a temporary scattering of their flock to the Netherlands, there returned thence during James I's reign, Henry Jacob, who was to set up at Southwark in 1616 the first Congregational church to maintain a continuous existence.

From the same root of Separatism there stemmed the English Baptists, bearing evident affinities with the Anabaptists of the continent in many respects, though not of direct affiliation. 'The father and founder of the organized Baptists of England and of the General Baptists in particular,' John Smyth, had been successively an Anglican clergyman and minister of an Independent church, before parting from the latter on the issue of infant baptism. Becoming convinced that the Church must be constituted only on the basis of the baptism of professed believers, he proceeded first to rebaptize himself, and then all his congregation, while still in exile at Amsterdam. In the method of baptism however he was traditional, using affusion from a basin, not immersion. Equally important was his espousal of the Arminian opinion that Christ died for all, in opposition to the predominant Calvinist doctrine that Christ died only for the elect. Actually the first church of English Baptists was thus founded on foreign soil; and to one of Smyth's followers, Thomas Helwys, a lawyer and layman, fell the honour of establishing the first Baptist church in England at Spitalfields in 1612. Moreover, both Smyth and Helwys were pioneers in their enunciation of the principle of religious toleration and freedom of conscience. Smyth, in denying the right of the magistrate to compel adherence to any church, insisted that he must 'leave the Christian religion free to every man's conscience', since 'Christ only is the king and lawgiver of the church and conscience'. Similarly Helwys affirmed that 'men's religion to God is betwixt God and themselves; the king shall not answer for it, neither may the king be judge between God and man'. Here was a new voice, as yet little heeded, but pregnant with hope for the future. Almost a generation later, between 1633 and 1638, there appeared the Particular or Calvinistic Baptists, emerging as a secession from Independency on the issue of infant baptism; and practising from the first baptism by immersion, in which they were shortly followed by the General Baptists.

The emergence of a Separatist movement within Puritanism was a portent, which drew Anglicans and Presbyterians closer together (as evidenced by the later career of Thomas Cartwright), against the extremes of Independent and Baptist. For in public worship the Separatists insisted on free or extemporary prayer against the episcopalian and presbyterian demand for a fixed liturgy; whilst they were pioneers of church democracy against the hierarchical constitution of Anglican and Presbyterian. The phenomenon from which Archbishop Matthew Parker had prayed to be delivered, 'the people to be the orderers of things' had come to pass. Even more important perhaps, the upholders of the 'gathered' church had thrown down the gauntlet to Caesar in behalf of God, and had defied the claim of *Leviathan* to control the conscience of man. The answer to Hobbes or to Hitler had been given by anticipation in the lives and deaths of Barrowe, Greenwood, and Penry.

8. THE ROMAN CATHOLICS

'THOU and I are priests,' said Blessed John Boste to John Ballard, who was about to suffer execution for treason with Antony Babington for plotting against the queen: 'It is our function to invade souls; and not to meddle with these temporal invasions; they belong not to us.' How much of the tragic story of the persecution of Roman Catholics during the reign of Elizabeth I is epitomized in these words! For the church settlement, which she had designed to be a means of cementing national unity and a focus of loyalty, failed to commend itself to many defenders of 'the old religion', as well as to Puritan zealots. At first, indeed, Elizabeth aspired to draw conservatives into the fold of her national establishment. She even hoped to attract some of the Marian bishops to accept her modified oath of supremacy; and particular hopes were held of the venerable Cuthbert Tunstall, Bishop of Durham, who was a survivor from the days of the pre-Henrician schism. Even after their disappointment, the deprived Marian prelates were treated with comparative lenity and mildness. Nor should the fact be forgotten, for it is of great significance, that between 1559 and 1570 no Recusant was put to death for religion. During this period the religious situation was fluctuating and uncertain. Not until the Council of Trent had finished its work in December, 1563, was the position of Rome itself clearly and sharply defined; and after that the papacy tarried still in the hope of a reversal of the position in England.

Finally, however, in 1570 by the Bull *Regnans in Excelsis*, Pius V not only declared Elizabeth I to be a heretic and religious communion with her Church to be forbidden, but also deprived her of the right to her kingdom, and absolved all her subjects from allegiance to her. The sentence of ecclesiastical excommunication was just and proper from the standpoint of Rome; and had been long expected. The fatal and crucial part was her deposition, and the absolution of her subjects from their civil allegiance to her as queen. 'Never since 1570,' observes a modern Roman Catholic historian, 'has any Pope excommunicated any sovereign in such a way as to declare the subjects free from their allegiance, and bound to rebel'; and when in 1572 Gregory XIII became pope, the same writer affirms of him that he 'set himself to a systematic effort, that only ended with his life, to dethrone Elizabeth by force of arms'. The Bull had followed an abortive rising in the north of England; and was shortly to be itself followed by the massacre of Huguenots in France on St. Bartholomew's Day, 1572. It inaugurated, moreover, in England a series of assassination-plots against the queen, which culminated in the attempted invasion of the country by the Spanish Armada. On its side, Elizabeth I's government and parliament replied with a series of punitive and penal statutes against Roman Catholic proselytes and proselytisers, of ever-increasing severity; and with a rigorous execution of these measures. From the purely political standpoint, those who had called for the sword were to perish by the sword; and for this Rome must bear the chief responsibility by the terms of the bull of excommunication.

Unfortunately it was impossible to sever purely religious from compromising political issues; and some martyrs for religion perished together with rebels and plotters. For the Society of Jesus, founded in 1540, was to become the spearhead of the Counter-Reformation movement; and its intrepid apostles were resolved to reclaim heretic England for the Roman obedience. Moreover a Lancashireman, William Allen, had established in the new university of Douai a college to train priests for the English mission from which by the end of Elizabeth I's reign there had gone forth 450 men for this work. This was followed later by the English College in Rome; and when to these missionaries there was joined a small band of Jesuits, the stage was set for a sustained campaign for the recovery of England. Two of these Jesuits, Edmund Campion and Robert Persons were typical respectively of the purely religious and partly political sides of the confused struggle. Campion was martyred, and Persons escaped. At the scaffold Campion affirmed his loyalty to the queen, 'unto whom I wish a long, quiet reign, with all prosperity'; and his purely religious aims: 'I am a Catholic man and a priest; in that faith I have lived, and in that faith I intend to die. If you esteem my religion treason, then I am guilty; as for other treason, I never committed any, God is my judge.' Many more martyrs were added during the later years of the reign, and not only priests. Indeed the crushing to death on the old Ouse bridge at York of Margaret Clitheroe remains one of the most moving and terrible episodes of persecution.

The primary duty of the missionary priests was to administer the sacraments and confirm the faith of their fellow-religionists, who were increasingly restricted by punitive laws, and cut off from social intercourse and public life. Such conditions produced many temptations to apostasy; and Roman Catholicism, alike for clergy and laity, became for two centuries and a half what Newman found it in the early nineteenth century, the religion of a *gens lucifuga*, a proscribed and hidden cult. Unfortunately, there developed sharp differences between the secular and regular priests concerning the administration of the affairs of the dwindling Roman household of faith. As the course of political events demonstrated the improbability of the overthrow of Elizabeth I by foreign invasion or domestic rebellion, a moderate party would have been glad to come to terms with the temporal power, by accepting an oath of allegiance, and renouncing the papal claim to depose heretic rulers and to dispense their subjects from civil loyalty. But the bull of 1570 hung like a millstone round the necks of the moderates;

and the extreme party had no desire for its rescinding. More serious was the quarrel concerning the provision of bishops for the scattered flock in England. The greater the persecution, ostracism, and isolation of the faithful, the more urgent would appear the need of bishops to administer the rite of Confirmation, to supervise the clergy, and to strengthen the steadfastness of the laity. But the Jesuits in particular had no wish for the restraining powers of a bishop; and they urged the laity to petition against the despatch of bishops to England, arguing for the superior advantages of direct dependence on the papacy. Hence resulted the disconcerting vacillations of papal policy. In 1580 one of the two surviving Marian bishops, the septuagenarian Goldwell of St. Asaph, was ordered to return to England, but died on the journey. For nearly a quarter of a century now the Jesuits had their way; and Arch-priests were appointed with authority only over the secular clergy and without commission to perform any properly episcopal functions. In 1622 another septuagenarian bishop was sent; and after his early death, Richard Smith, Bishop of Chalcedon, ruled from 1625 to 1631. After his departure, the Roman Catholics were left for another fifty years, until the reign of James II, without bishops; and this during one of the most difficult of all periods of their history.

Throughout the sixteenth and seventeenth centuries therefore the Roman Catholic recusants suffered from the inextricable association of their religious profession with political disloyalty. Nor were they fortunate in the attempts of kings to alleviate their lot. The initial favour of James I was followed by severe persecution after the discovery of the Gunpowder Plot; that of Charles II led to the horrors of the Popish Plot, and the open championship of James II led to a still sharper reaction which excluded them from the benefits of the Toleration Act of 1689. Thus persecution and temptations to apostasy were multiplied; and the Roman Catholics passed into the cave and the tunnel. Some succumbed to the pressing advantages of apostasy; others stood firm; and little, isolated groups of the faithful gathered round the houses of such of the nobility and gentry as defied ostracism, fines, and persecution. Indeed the survival and persistence of the Roman Catholic faith until the coming of Emancipation in 1829 is a story of heroism, pathos, and schism. Many indeed had trial of bonds and imprisonment; for the legacy of Pius V's bull of excommunication was to visit the sins of the fathers upon the children until more than the third and fourth generations of English Romanists.

9. THE GROWTH OF THE ANGLICAN TRADITION

In my last three talks I sketched the challenge to the Church of England from Presbyterian, Independent, and Roman Catholic. It is proper now to examine the effects of this protracted struggle on the character and tradition of that Church itself. For in the crucible of controversy Anglicanism as a positive version of Christianity was hammered out. In part the outward circumstances of this development were created by the providential length of the reign of Elizabeth I and by her staunch opposition to all attempts to overthrow her religious settlement. With the defeat of these various and successive assaults, the Church of England was able to stand forth in fact as well as in aspiration as a *via media* between Rome and Geneva.

In the first place, the *Ecclesia Anglicana* threw off the strait-waistcoat of Calvinism which had been dominant in its theology during the greater part of the queen's long reign. Hooker himself indeed affirmed that 'of what account the Master of the Sentences was in the Church of Rome, the same and more amongst the preachers of the Reformed Churches Calvin had purchased, so that the perfectest divines were judged they which were the skilfullest in Calvin's writings'. Nor was this estimate exaggerated. Archbishop Whitgift, for example, the harshest *malleus Puritanorum*, was at one with his adversaries on theological issues; and his victims on their part could subscribe without difficulty to the doctrinal articles of the Thirty-Nine Articles. Indeed when the foundations of Calvin's doctrine were threatened at Cambridge by the attack of Peter Baro on predestination, Whitgift drew up, in 1595, a series of Lambeth Articles which, if they had received the royal assent, would have enforced a strictly Calvinist interpretation of the Thirty-Nine Articles as the only orthodox position. With, however, the growth of a new school of theology, called after the Dutch divine Arminius, a more liberal and comprehensive attitude prevailed. The Church of England became content to allow many open questions in theology, especially those relating to the dark mysteries of predestination and election, and to hold fast to the fundamentals of the faith as stated in the three creeds.

With this emancipation from a rigid dogmatism, there went an emphasis on the beauty of holiness as expressed in public worship. It is unfortunate that the epithet of 'Laudian' has become inseparably associated with the Arminian tradition in England; for Laud has had an unusually bad press. Even G. M. Trevelyan has described him as 'this Richelieu of religion'. The tribute of S. R. Gardiner is more just. 'It is little,' he wrote of Laud, 'that every parish church in the land still . . . presents a spectacle which realizes his hopes. It is far more that his refusal to submit his mind to the dogmatism of Puritanism and his appeal to the cultivated intelligence for the solution of religious problems, has received an ever-increasing response, even in regions where his memory is devoted to contemptuous obloquy.' If Laud stood for a fixed liturgy and uniformity of rites and ceremonies, he championed also a free pulpit; whilst his opponents stood for a free liturgy and a rigid theological system. The Laudians wished to restore the services of the Prayer Book to the standard of decorum and reverence laid down in its rubrics. Thus they wished to enforce the wearing of the surplice in parish churches, and the cope in cathedrals; to restore the Communion Table to the traditional position of the medieval altar, 'sideway under the east window of every chancel or chapel', and to protect it from profanation by rails; and to require communicants to receive the sacrament kneeling. In cathedrals they encouraged the celebration of the Eucharist with solemn music and stately ceremonial, including altar lights and richly-adorned vestments. Moreover, in such books of devotion as Lancelot Andrewes' *Preces Privatae*, the Eucharist became once again the focus of prayer and piety.

As the Church of England recovered its catholic heritage in rites and ceremonies, so also it came to a new estimation of episcopacy. During the Presbyterian controversy, it had become conscious of the historic tradition and positive value of episcopacy, and it rejoiced in its superior fortune to many reformed Churches of the continent in the careful retention of episcopal succession and government. Leading divines of the new school indeed, such as Lancelot Andrewes and John Bramhall, following the example of Hooker and Whitgift, would not pronounce episcopacy to be of the *esse* of the Church in such wise as to unchurch the Presbyterian Churches of Europe; but they certainly regarded it as necessary to the wholeness or completeness of the Church. In this they were encouraged by new contacts which individual Anglicans were making with the Eastern Orthodox Churches. With the foundation of the Levant Company in 1599 and the expansion of trade with the middle east, Anglican chaplains came into closer touch with the Eastern Orthodox Churches; and during the Commonwealth period these contacts were increased by a number of exiled clerics. Archdeacon Basire, for example, deserved the eulogy of John Evelyn as 'that great traveller, or rather French apostle, who had been planting the Church of England in divers parts of the Levant and Asia'. Anglicans were not slow to see points of similarity with these ancient Churches, determinedly hostile to Rome yet preserving episcopacy and a venerable liturgy, and untouched moreover by the storms of the western Reformation. Thus the Church of England became increasingly resolved to emphasize its links with the past in its own Book of Common Prayer and its episcopal order and government.

Perhaps the best illustration of this new Anglican school may be seen in the translation of its principles into terms of pastoral cure in *The Priest to the Temple* of George Herbert at Bemerton, near Salisbury. Of Sunday duty he wrote that his country parson 'having read divine service twice fully, and preached in the morning and catechized in the afternoon, he thinks he hath in some measure . . . discharged the public duties of the congregation'. The rest of the day he spent in visiting his parishioners and enjoying with them innocent social recreation. The Holy Communion, he held, should be celebrated, 'if not duly once a month, yet at least five or six times in the year; as at Easter, Christmas, Whitsuntide, and afore and after harvest and beginning of Lent'. He was diligent in visiting his flock, both in sickness and health, in teaching his children the Prayer Book catechism; and at home he observed days of fasting as a private discipline. He insisted that in his parish church 'all things there be decent', as became the service of God; such as 'the walls plaistered, windows glazed, floors paved, and seats whole, firm, and uniform'. In particular he was careful 'that the pulpit, desk and communion-table be as they ought'; and that the east end had 'fit and proper texts of scripture everywhere painted'. On great festivals the church was 'strawed and struck with boughs and perfumed with incense'. The due balance between the ministries of the Word and Sacraments was kept by his description of his pulpit as 'his joy and his throne'; where, in regard to the frailty of his people, 'he exceeds not an hour in preaching, because all ages have thought that a competency'.

Thus from the ornate and splendid ceremonial of Durham Cathedral under Dean Cosin to the village church of Bemerton under Herbert, the Laudians sought to recall their fellow-churchmen to a dignified and seemly order of public worship. They found no contradiction in proclaiming themselves at once both Catholic and Protestant. Archbishop Laud in his last Will professed his resolve to die, 'as he had lived, in the true, orthodox profession of the Catholic faith of Christ, a true member of his Catholic Church, within the communion of a living part thereof, the present Church of England'. So in his last words on the scaffold he affirmed that he 'had always lived in the Protestant religion established in England and in that he now came to die'. Similarly Bishop Andrewes prayed 'for the Catholic Church, its confirmation and enlargement; for the Eastern, its deliverance and unity; for the Western, its adjustment and peace; for the British, the supply of what is wanting and the establishment of what remains'. Such was the ideal expressed also in Herbert's poem *The British Church.*

I joy, dear Mother, when I view
Thy perfect lineaments and hue,
Both sweet and bright.

Beauty in thee takes up her place,
And dates her letters from thy face,
When she doth write.

A fine aspect, in fit array,
Neither too mean, nor yet too gay,
Shews who is best.

Outlandish looks may not compare,
For all they either painted are,
Or else undrest.

But dearest Mother (what those miss)
The mean thy praise and glory is,
And long may be.

10. THE TRIUMPH OF PURITANISM

ALTHOUGH the policy of tarrying for the magistrate had paid such slender dividends during the long reign of Elizabeth I, the conforming Presbyterians did not lose heart. The queen was not immortal; and, after the execution of Mary Queen of Scots in 1587, it became clear that Elizabeth I's successor would be James of Scotland; and what might not be hoped from a king brought up in Presbyterian surroundings? Accordingly on James' accession, the Millenary Petition was presented to him, containing the requests of the Presbyterian clergy. It was as significant for what it did not ask, as for what it did. The petitioners were at pains to assure the king that they were 'neither factious men, affecting a popular parity in the Church, nor schismatics aiming at the dissolution of the state ecclesiastical'. That is, they were neither Brownists, nor even adherents of the programme of the *Admonitions to Parliament* of thirty years ago! Instead they asked mainly for 'the redress of divers abuses of the church'; particularly those which arose from their 'groaning under a common burden of human rites and ceremonies'. They desired the omission of such 'nocent ceremonies' as the cross in baptism, the ring in marriage, bowing at the name of Jesus, and the wearing of the surplice; whilst positively they asked for a preaching ministry, its better maintenance, and for the restoration of ecclesiastical discipline. At the Hampton Court Conference, summoned to hear and debate their case, the king came down decisively on the side of the Episcopalians. Henceforth the Presbyterians had to abide patiently through the coming Laudian regime, observing the minimum of conformity necessary to retain their benefices, and tarrying the Lord's leisure as well as that of the magistrate.

With the outbreak of civil war between Charles I and Parliament their day of triumph seemed at long last to have come. For bishops were first excluded from the House of Lords; and then both episcopacy and the Book of Common Prayer were proscribed. Moreover, when in 1643 the parliamentary party sought the alliance of the Scots, one of the conditions of this military help was the reformation of the Church of England 'according to the pattern of the best reformed churches'. Thus the Westminster Assembly was summoned in July, 1643, to effect this task; and now patience was to have her perfect work. Now, too, the hidden strength of the Presbyterian conformists became evident; as the company of grave clergymen assembled, ordained episcopally under Elizabeth I and James I, and having held on in the hope of such a day as this. The synod consisted of thirty lay assessors, chosen from both Houses of Parliament, 121 English divines, including five Independents and some of known episcopalian sympathies, and eight Scottish commissioners. Upon any reckoning it is one of the most important English ecclesiastical assemblies. It produced the Westminster Confession of Faith, still the ruling standard of the Presbyterian Church in England; the Larger and Shorter Catechisms, the latter of which particularly has won widespread acceptance on its merits; and a Directory for the Public Worship of God, representing 'a *via media* between a prescribed liturgy and extemporaneous prayer'. These were very considerable achievements; and if the parallel schemes for ordination and the establishment of the godly discipline did not take effect, this was due to the changing military and political situation. In the opinion of Richard Baxter, the most learned and renowned of English Presbyterians of the age, 'the Christian world since the days of the apostles had never had a synod of more excellent divines (taking one thing with another) than this synod and the Synod of Dort were'.

Other observers indeed took a less favourable view. John Milton was representative of a growing minority of Independent opinion, which was convinced that 'new Presbyter is but old Priest writ large'; and that the Westminster Assembly would produce no greater toleration and liberty than a Laudian convocation. Indeed, he averred that it was characterized by 'plots and packing worse than Trent'. The influence of this minority opinion was to be greatly enhanced by the fortunes of war. For the decisive element in the parliamentary victory over the crown was to be Cromwell's Eastern Association and New Model armies; in which Independency and toleration were the religious watchwords. Moreover, the first civil war was the prelude to a second; after which the forces of moderation, alike in Church and State, were eclipsed. Charles I was executed, and a Commonwealth proclaimed, which issued shortly in the military Protectorate of Oliver Cromwell himself. Naturally, the Protector was vitally interested in the religious settlement; and if he proved himself in some respects more tolerant than the majority of his followers, as in his administrative favours to Quakers and Jews, in other respects he was more conservative, as in his insistence on retaining compulsory payment of tithe and church dues for the maintenance of the ministry against the champions of voluntary remuneration only.

But if Cromwell retained the territorial parish system, he needed to provide some central administration and control of the Church. Neither Episcopacy nor Presbyterianism could be stomached by his followers. Yet some means must be evolved of admitting persons to benefices, and of dismissing them. The means adopted was that of a national Committee of Triers and local Committees of Ejectors. The latter did their work of preparation by getting rid of unsuitable incumbents, to the number of between 6,000 and 7,000; a circumstance worthy of recollection when the reverse process was effected at the Stuart restoration. The Committee of Triers filled the vacancies thus created; and their certificate was essential for admission to a benefice. They judged not by theological orthodoxy, nor according to any particular method of ordination. They were concerned with evidence of a godly life and reliable political opinions. Thus the ministry was composed chiefly of Presbyterian, Independent, and Baptist pastors; though a considerable number of Episcopalians retained their livings, on condition that they did not use the Common Prayer services from the Book, though no one could prevent their saying them by heart. Cromwell himself dispensed the patronage formerly in the gift of the crown; and private patronage was undisturbed; though all ministers needed the *imprimatur* of the Committee of Triers. Thus a national establishment of Christianity was maintained, held together by the power of the Protector and his Committees, but otherwise divided in points of theology and ordination. It was a remarkable and unprecedented experiment in comprehension; and outside its latitude, Cromwell did his best to give practical toleration by administrative measures to the extreme sects, especially the Quakers. Baxter, indeed, gave it as his considered opinion that the Triers 'did abundance of good to the Church; they saved many a congregation from ignorant, ungodly, drunken teachers, . . . and that sort of Ministers that either preacht against a holy Life, or preacht as men that never were acquainted with it; . . . and in their stead admitted of any that were able, serious Preachers, and lived a godly life, of what tolerable opinion soever they were'.

Notwithstanding, the ecclesiastical settlement was a house divided against itself; and its duration depended upon Cromwell's life. With his death in 1658, its days were numbered. But despite the brevity of its experiment, the influence of the Commonwealth period in religion was far-reaching and important. First, the numbers of Presbyterians, Independents, and Baptists had so multiplied that, in the aggregate and if they combined together, they constituted a body of opinion to which toleration could not be ultimately denied. This was the most important consequence of the Interregnum. Secondly, it established the Presbyterians as by far the strongest body of Protestants outside the episcopalian system. Indeed with the return of the Long Parliament to authority and office after the collapse of the Protectorate, it seemed as if the Presbyterians had the game in their hands; since no restoration of the Stuart monarchy could be effected without their support; and they might attach what religious conditions they would to their offer of support. Finally, the Commonwealth had seen developed to their fullest extent the principles of democracy, first set forth by the Independents in the reign of Elizabeth I. Church democracy had now led to political democracy; and the Bible, after being the pattern for ecclesiastical self-government, had become the text-book of radical political theories. For better and for worse the Tudor theory of the identity of Church and State had been finally shattered; and the future pattern of English religious and political life was never to approach the ideal of *ein Reich, ein Völk, eine Kirche.* This perhaps was the greatest legacy of the Commonwealth; and its basis had been religious, fashioned by and on the English Bible, of the influence of which on the seventeenth century Englishman I shall speak in my next talk.

11. THE ENGLISH BIBLE

'THE Bible, I say, the Bible only is the religion of Protestants'. This avowal of William Chillingworth, an Anglican divine who had been converted to Rome and then had returned to his former allegiance, might be taken as epitomizing English religion during the seventeenth century. For that century was *par excellence* the age of the English Bible. One of the most satisfactory results of the Hampton Court Conference was the production of the Authorized Version, the influence of which it is as difficult to describe as to exaggerate. In the prose of John Milton and John Bunyan, and in the speech of Oliver Cromwell, its potency is evident so that he who runs may read. More intangible, but not less real, was its part in fashioning domestic piety, as the head of a household gathered his family on the Lord's Day for the reading of the Scriptures, in moulding the moral standards of earnest Christians; and in setting, as was believed, a model also for the form of political government. But above all, of course, it was the text-book of Christian belief and theology.

The insistence upon the authority of the Bible as the sole basis of belief and profession had been an outstanding characteristic of the sixteenth century reformers. They had assumed, however, that the Bible would be its own interpreter, if read apart from the refracting medium of the traditions of the Church. Shortly this facile assumption was proved to be wrong. Luther, Zwingli, and Calvin could not agree in their doctrine of the Eucharist; Anglican and Presbyterian were at variance over the form of church government most consonant with the evidence of the New Testament, whilst Independents contradicted both. Much more ominous, there appeared a sect of Socinians which threw doubt on the traditional doctrine of the Trinity, and set forth plainly heretical views on this cardinal touchstone of othodoxy. Where then was the arbiter when doctors of the reformed tradition disagreed in their exegesis of the Word of God? Perhaps the most remarkable phenomenon of the seventeenth century was the emphasis given to the office and work of the Holy Spirit in making plain the counsels of God. In its most moderate form, this doctrine was expressed by John Robinson in his farewell oration to the Pilgrim Fathers; 'if God reveal anything to you by any other instrument of His, be as ready to receive it as you were to receive any truth by my ministry; for I am verily persuaded the Lord hath more truth yet to break forth out of His holy word'. Cromwell held that God 'speaks without a written word sometimes, yet according to it'. But others were not content with this position. Conscious of the immediate promptings of the Spirit, they tended to 'try the Scriptures by the Spirit, and not the Spirit by the Scriptures'.

Perhaps the most striking example of this appeal to the Spirit was the emergence of the Quakers. George Fox indeed had tried various of the denominations of the Commonwealth and found each unsatisfactory in turn, before attaining to his discovery and doctrine of the Inner Light as the solution of all mysteries. 'When all my hopes in them and all men were gone, so that I had nothing outwardly to help me, nor could I tell what to do, then I heard a voice which said: "There is one, Christ Jesus, that can speak to thy condition"; and when I heard it my heart did leap for joy.' Like John Wesley in the following century, he travelled widely not only in these islands but in New England, to proclaim his gospel of the Inner Light. His followers were abhorred by most Protestants; for they had neither church, ministry, nor sacraments; and popular ridicule was incurred by their curious eccentricities of speech and dress. Notwithstanding, Fox laid the basis of an experimental knowledge of the Holy Spirit, and founded a Society, which has been remarkably fecund in good works and in philanthropic enterprises of various kinds.

The seventeenth century indeed was an epoch of great leaders. Richard Baxter, whose description of himself as a 'meer Catholick' is exactly pertinent, was eminent as preacher, organizer, theologian and casuist. An earnest seeker for unity, he gathered all the Protestant denominations of Worcestershire into an ecclesiastical Association in 1653. He desired to make the Apostles' Creed the sole test of belief, the Lord's Prayer a sufficient summary of devotion and the Ten Commandments of duty; and to embrace all persons willing to accept these standards as members of one catholic Church. Moreover he was a prolific writer; whose *Reformed Pastor* became the manual of pastoral theology of his times; whose *Christian Directory* was a text-book of moral theology for Protestant divines; and whose *Saints' Everlasting Rest* was a classic of devotion, excelled only by the greater work of Bunyan. To a remarkable extent Baxter stood aloof from, even above, the controversies of his age; and at the restoration he was offered a bishopric, but declined. In the conflict of Spirit versus Scriptures, he held stoutly to the traditional position: 'We must prefer the Spirit's inspiring the apostles to indite the Scriptures, before the Spirit's illuminating of us to understand them, or before any present inspirations. . . . This trying the Spirit by the Scriptures, is not a setting of the Scriptures above the Spirit itself; but it is only a trying of the Spirit by the Spirit.'

More popular and widely known however than Baxter's writings is the *Pilgrim's Progress* by John Bunyan, in which the epitome of the influence of the English Bible may be seen. Like his other masterpiece, *Grace Abounding*, it was written in prison at Bedford after the restoration; and it has been called by Sir Charles Firth 'the prose epic of English Puritanism'. Its limpid prose, its Biblical language and imagery, and its moving yet homely allegory of the journey of Christian from the city of destruction to the celestial city, made it a classic of popular religion. 'It addressed the unlettered Puritan,' as Firth observed, 'in a speech which unlettered Puritans could understand. The people for whom Bunyan wrote were illiterate people like his pilgrims themselves. . . . But they knew their Bible well, and were never at a loss for a text. They could follow Bunyan in his highest flights, and in his most serious theological arguments, because he used the language of the Bible, and adopted its words, its phrases, and its imagery. Bunyan's English is the English of the Bible.'

But if *Pilgrim's Progress* was written for the unlettered, John Milton set forth theology for the learned, both in prose and verse. From his earlier poems, *L'Allegro, Il Penseroso,* and *Lycidas*, to his later and more sombre epics, *Paradise Lost, Samson Agonistes*, and *Paradise Regained*, in which he essayed the ambitious task 'to justify the ways of God to man', he represented the embodiment of Puritan culture wedded to piety. No religious tradition which numbered him amongst its defenders need be ashamed to speak with its enemies in the gate. Nor was he alone among Puritans in his combination of sound learning with earnest religion. In Oxford John Owen, Dean of Christ Church and Vice-Chancellor of the university during the Interregnum, was a scholar not unworthy of such high offices; and at Cambridge Peter Sterry of Emmanuel College likewise found no incompatibility between culture and Christianity.

Thus the influence of the English Bible was all-pervasive during the seventeenth century. Since the beginning of Elizabeth I's reign lessons from its Old and New Testaments had been read in parish churches at Morning and Evening Prayer every Sunday. During her reign also the Genevan Bible had nourished personal and individual piety, thanks largely to its small size which made it convenient for reading at home. In 1611 the Authorized Version was published, and soon established its popularity against all rivals. No aspect of English life at this time can be understood without reference to the Bible. The speeches of Oliver Cromwell read more like sermons than parliamentary orations; and for this reason modern Englishmen find Cromwell an enigma. The advanced social programmes of the Levellers were founded on texts from the Bible. The high churchman George Herbert, not less than Baxter or Bunyan, found 'the chief and top of his knowledge in the book of books, the storehouse and magazine of life and comfort, the Holy Scriptures', wherein he valued especially 'four things: precepts for life, doctrines for knowledge, examples for illustration, and promises for comfort'. The Covenant relationship which was the basis of Independent church polity found its secular counterpart in the doctrine of a Social Contract as the foundation of civil society. On all sides, the verdict of a historian of an older generation, John Richard Green, on the seventeenth century, stands firm, that 'England became the people of a book, and that book was the Bible'.

12. THE PARTING OF THE WAYS

DURING the hundred years dividing the accession of Elizabeth I from the restoration of Charles II, the religious situation in England had undergone many vicissitudes. The Elizabethan settlement had been assailed by Presbyterian and Separatist, had repulsed their assaults and had seemed to be settling down to a period of quiet development; and then had come the rude shock of the victory first of the Presbyterians in the Westminster Assembly and then of Independency under the Protectorate. After the death of Oliver Cromwell had presaged the return of the Stuarts, the stage seemed set for a definite settlement of the religious and ecclesiastical issues; but what kind of settlement was difficult to predict. Both in the returning Long Parliament, which effected the recall of the king, and in the Convention Parliament elected to work out the details of the restoration, the Presbyterians possessed a majority. It seemed therefore as if Charles II could only return to his throne on their conditions. Chastened by their experiences during the Commonwealth, they were predisposed to seek a solution along the lines of 'Comprehension'; that is, the making of such changes in the Book of Common Prayer and in the operation of episcopacy as would comprehend Presbyterian and Episcopalian within the fold of one, national, and established Church. Had they insisted on this as a condition of the king's return, it is difficult to see how it could have been denied. Instead, Charles was allowed to come back simply on the terms of the Declaration of Breda, which promised 'a liberty to tender consciences, and that no man shall be disquieted or called in question for differences of opinion in matters of religion, which do not disturb the peace of the kingdom', subject to a future act of parliament 'for the full granting of that indulgence'. Consequently, the religious settlement was determined by the company of Anglican bishops and clergy who had eaten the bitter bread of banishment with Charles rather than bow themselves in the Commonwealth House of Rimmon; and the Presbyterians found themselves excluded equally with the Independents, from the restored national Church.

The fundamental mistake of the Presbyterians was to allow the political settlement so far to take precedence of the ecclesiastical as to lead to the dissolution of the Convention Parliament after the first part only had been effected. The resultant election of the fervently royalist and Anglican Cavalier Parliament left no doubt of the nature of the religious settlement. The returned Anglican exiles, supported by Edward Hyde, the king's principal minister, played a skilful delaying game. Charles II in his *Declaration concerning Ecclesiastical Affairs*, of October 1660, complimented 'the most able and principal assertors of the presbyterian opinions' on their being 'full of zeal for the peace of the church and state, and neither enemies . . . to episcopacy or liturgy, but modestly to desire such alterations in either as, without shaking foundations, might best allay the present distempers'. Accordingly he held out hopes of such changes as the compulsory association of presbyters with bishops in the administrative and judicial duties of the episcopal office; the revision of the Canon Law; and the permissive disuse of the surplice and of the 'nocent ceremonies' until an agreed settlement was reached. Bishoprics were thereupon offered to Baxter, Calamy, and Reynolds (the last named accepting Norwich on the terms of the Declaration); and a conference was promised to work out the details of the 'comprehension'.

Whilst the political issues were being determined, however, the bishops resumed their seats in the House of Lords, vacant sees were filled, cathedral chapters returned to their heritage, and the Canterbury Convocation was summoned. When therefore the promised conference between Episcopalians and Presbyterians met at the Savoy in 1661, the Anglicans were already in possession of the Church; and the Presbyterians were in the position of suppliants. The Prayer Book revision was undertaken in fact by the Convocations, and accepted without detailed debate by Parliament. By the Act of Uniformity of 1662, episcopal ordination was made essential for all ministers of the established Church, and all clergy had to take an oath of 'unfeigned assent and consent to all and everything contained and prescribed in' the revised Prayer Book by St. Bartholomew's Day (August 24). The result was that about 1,760 incumbents were ejected from their livings. Moreover, worse was to ensue in the persecuting measures of the miscalled 'Clarendon Code', which followed up the extrusion of Presbyterians and Independents from the re-established Church by attempting to suppress dissent altogether. In the restoration settlement of the Church, the English religious tradition had reached the parting of the ways. The wheel had turned full circle; and the century-long conflict between episcopacy and presbytery had been finally determined within the Church of England in favour of the former.

Two very important consequences followed for the future religious development of England. First, the Presbyterians henceforth made common cause with the Independents and Baptists. Although the Presbyterians retained for more than a generation their desire for 'comprehension', and various schemes to this end were privately discussed and even a formal attempt made in 1689 to carry them into effect, though in vain, this desire was always accompanied by the demand for an 'indulgence' for their fellow-dissenters. In 1689 the Toleration Act was passed, and comprehension finally disappeared from the field of practical politics. The toleration thus granted however was limited and meagre. The very title of the statute was chilling; 'an act to exempt their majesties' Protestant subjects dissenting from the Church of England from the penalties of certain laws'. It granted freedom of public worship to orthodox, that is Trinitarian, Protestant Dissenters, on condition that their meeting houses were registered with the appropriate authorities of either Church or State, that their meetings for worship were held with open doors, and that their ministers subscribed the doctrinal articles of the Thirty-Nine Articles. No attempt was made to relax, or remove, the civil disabilities of Dissenters. Not until 1779 was a form of subscription expressing simple belief in the authority of the Bible substituted for that of the Anglican Articles of Religion; and not till 1813 were Unitarians allowed to shelter under the protection of the Toleration Act. Notwithstanding, toleration once granted, was never withdrawn; and in this as in many other aspects of English development, *c'est le premier pas qui coûte*.

Secondly, the effects of 1662 and 1689 upon the social and political, as well as religious, history of England were to be profound and far-reaching. Protestant Dissenters had to accept a position of civic and social inferiority which lasted until the middle of the nineteenth century; and the social divisions between Anglicans and Dissenters were to be deeper and more difficult to bridge than the theological and ecclesiastical. In particular, the Dissenters had to provide means of higher education for their ministers and for the children of their church members, of which more must be said later. Contemporaneously also with the parting of the ways in ecclesiastical matters there developed the organization of the rival political parties of Whig and Tory in the State; and in view of their civil disabilities, the Dissenters gravitated naturally into alliance with the Whigs. The consequences of this religico-political affiliation were to be of great importance during the nineteenth century. Finally, in the ecclesiastical sphere, the legal recognition of the Protestant Dissenting churches perpetuated the problem of episcopalian and non-episcopalian ordinations, which remains unsolved in the present century. The Restoration Church settlement, therefore, for better and for worse, marked the parting of the ways in England. A ' comprehension ' might have reduced the Independents and Baptists to a comparatively insignificant minority, and delayed the advent of toleration. Instead, the failure of comprehension and the victory of toleration (partial and restricted though it was) opened a great door and was effectual in the future history and development of the English religious tradition.

13. THE INTELLECTUAL REVOLUTION

'It is plain to me,' wrote John Locke in his *Essay concerning Human Understanding*, ' we have a more certain knowledge of the existence of a God, than of anything our senses have not immediately discovered to us. Nay, I presume to say, that we more certainly know that there is a God, than that there is anything else without us.' These words might be regarded as the keynote of that profound revolution in thought which was taking place in the background of the latter half of the seventeenth century, and which was to affect profoundly theology as well as other departments of human thinking, not only in that but for all succeeding centuries. Such a far-reaching movement had, of course, many causes. But the principal factor was the discovery or popularization, within the space of a single generation, of the telescope, microscope, barometer, and thermometer. Upon the horizon of the little band of English savants who, from the tower of Wadham College, Oxford, surveyed the starry heavens, there burst the revelation of the works of God in creation; speaking with an universal and compelling voice, and testifying to an omnipotent and beneficent Creator. To the pioneers of this nascent scientific movement, the works of God were at least of equal, if not of greater, importance than the record in his Word, as evidence of his character and purpose. The poet Joseph Addison expressed the new evangel exactly.

The Spacious Firmament on high,
With all the blue ethereal sky
And spangled heavens, a shining Frame,
Their great Original proclaim.
Th' unwearied Sun from day to day
Does his Creator's power display,
And publishes to every land
The work of an almighty Hand.

What though in solemn silence, all
Move round the dark, terrestrial Ball?
What though no real voice nor sound
Amid their radiant orbs be found?
In Reason's ear they all rejoice
And utter forth a glorious voice,
For ever singing as they shine,
'The Hand that made us is Divine'.

For in place of the old, capricious universe, dominated by hosts of evil spirits, whose quirks at any moment might bring disaster to mankind, there was revealed now a visible creation governed by an unvarying law, and observing an irrefragable order. But law implied a lawgiver; and order on such a majestic scale argued a Creator of infinite power and wisdom. Nor was man abased by this discovery, as he was to be by the scientific revolution of the nineteenth century. Instead, his prestige was immensely flattered by the realization that he alone of the created universe had been privileged to enter into an understanding of the purpose and methods of God in creation. For a generation, as discovery followed discovery, educated men became as little children, engaged

> *in tireless play, attentively occupied with a world of wonders, so rich in toys and playthings that naked Nature were enough without the marvellous inventory of man.*

The novelty and variety of scientific discoveries seemed to establish conclusively not only the wisdom and power of God, but also His beneficence to man. To Locke and the leaders of this scientific movement, the existence and attributes of God were capable of proof, so that all rational beings henceforth could accept the fundamental articles of religion.

From this invasion of the province of theology by scientific concepts there followed also the vogue of Natural Religion. For the evidence thus adduced of the nature and purpose of God was open to men of all races, times, and places. Herein it contrasted favourably with the proofs of Revelation, which had been vouchsafed only to men of one generation, living at a particular time and place, and the records of which were wrapped up in sacred books, written in languages no longer understood by the people. Against the universality of this Natural Religion there came to be set the scandal of the particularity of Christianity. Moreover, from the contemplation of the starry heavens above, the champions of Natural Religion passed to that of the moral law, written, as they firmly believed, in the heart of every man; and likewise of universal range and validity. Indeed so far was God from having left Himself without witness within the mind of men, that He had implanted there the conviction of His existence, of the duty of men to worship Him, and to imitate His beneficence, and of a future state of rewards and punishments for mankind. Thus the traditional relationship between Revelation and Natural Religion was reversed; and instead of asking whether peoples who had not heard of Christ could be saved, the question became whether Christianity added anything necessary to salvation to the tenets of Natural Religion. Once again a poet, the Roman Catholic John Dryden, epitomized the contemporary vogue.

If the Gentiles (whom no Law inspir'd)
By Nature did what was by Law required:
They who the written Rule had never known
Were to themselves both Rule and Law alone.
To Nature's plain indictment they shall plead
And by their conscience be condemned or freed . . .
Then those who follow'd Reason's dictates right,
Liv'd up and lifted high their Natural Light,
With Socrates may see their Maker's Face
While thousand Rubrick Martyrs want a place.

There was generated therefore a movement, within all the churches and without, for the simplification of Christianity. To a generation wearied with religious wars and theological systems, the notion of a highest common factor between natural and revealed religion was instantly attractive. John Locke, the prophet of his age in this as in many other respects, set forth the simple proposition that Christianity might be reduced to one article of belief, that Jesus was the Messiah, whose advent had been foretold by prophecy and whose mission was attested by miracles. Christianity in fact was nothing more or less than a re-publication of Natural Religion, in terms adapted to the meanest understanding and with reinforced sanctions of a future heaven or hell. 'This,' as Locke again observed, 'is a religion suited to vulgar capacities, and the state of mankind in this world, destined to labour and to travail.' Such advocacy of a simplified Christianity fell upon receptive ears. During the earlier part of the seventeenth century indeed the school of Cambridge Platonists had sought in their academic milieu to commend Christianity rather as a way of life, combining reason, mysticism and morality, than as a corpus of dogma. They had sought to harmonize culture and piety, knowledge and faith, Platonism and Christianity. Their company numbered famous names, Ralph Cudworth, Benjamin Whichcote, John Smith, Henry More (all save one bred in that nursery of Puritanism, Emmanuel College); and their influence was as fragrant as far-reaching. What they had taught in the academy, Locke and his disciples proclaimed in the market-place; and in the process of transference, the doctrine lost much of its mysticism and beauty. Reason degenerated into common sense; personal religious experience into homespun morality; the venture of faith into a prudential calculation of profit and loss. Archbishop Tillotson, who set a new style of preaching as well as a new content of sermons, was typical of this tendency to reduce the Divine Benevolence into an easy good nature. 'For is it not really desirable,' he asked in one of his sermons, 'that there should be such a Being as takes particular care of each one of us, and delights to do us good, understands all our wants, and is able and willing to relieve us in our greatest straits when nothing else can? Is it not every man's interest that there should be such a Governor of the world as really designs our happiness, and hath omitted nothing that is necessary to it, as would govern us for our advantage, and will require nothing of us but what is for our good; and yet will infinitely reward us for the doing of that which is best for ourselves? And we have reason to believe God to be such a Being, if He be at all.' Notwithstanding this decline from the Cambridge Platonists, the revolution in religious thought, which was characterized particularly by its emphasis on the Divine Benevolence, became the parent of an outburst of practical philanthropy, of which I shall speak in my next talk, and which was one of the remarkable features of the late seventeenth and early eighteenth centuries in England.

14. PRACTICAL CHRISTIANITY

'PRACTICAL Christianity was its talent and delight,' observed Archbishop Tenison of his age, and in so saying, characterized its outstanding achievement. Hitherto what I have said of the English religious tradition has been chiefly concerned with church government and the differing traditions of life and thought within the several Churches. Little has been said of the impact of Christianity upon society and its problems. The 'practical Christianity' which Tenison admired was the direct outcome of the combined scientific and religious movement, of which I spoke in my last talk. For the discovery of uniform law and order in the universe led to the conclusion that the Creator had been inspired therein by an especial beneficence to man. Therefore 'the whole duty of man' was to copy this

Divine Benevolence in his relations with his fellows, and to give himself to works of charity and philanthropy. The primacy of charity over theology was epitomized by the poet Alexander Pope.

For modes of faith let graceless zealots fight,
His can't be wrong whose life is in the right.
In Faith and Hope the world will disagree
But all mankind's concern is charity.
All must be false that thwart this one great end,
And all of God that bless mankind or mend.

Two of the most signal manifestations of this practical Christianity were to be seen in the fields of education and hospitals. In the former sphere, the rise of the Dissenting Academies was a noteworthy milestone in the history of higher education in England. For though from one standpoint it was a consequence of the social divisions created by the Act of Uniformity and subsequent legislation, it represented also the influx of new ideas and principles into English pedagogy. The Protestant Dissenters had to discover some substitute for the universities of Oxford and Cambridge, which became close Anglican monopolies and were virtually barred to others than members of the established Church. Therefore a number of the ministers ejected in 1662 set up academies within their own houses. The history of these academies was often one of migration, to avoid the arm of the law; and some of them had a record as chequered as renowned. Like the medieval universities, they depended for their prosperity upon the learning of their teachers; and by 1689 they numbered at least twenty-three, and multiplied rapidly afterwards. They taught what might not inappropriately be called 'modern subjects'; including natural science, modern as well as classical languages, modern philosophy and history; and their medium of instruction was English rather than Latin. At a time when Aristotle still dominated the universities, these academies familiarized their students with the new philosophy of Descartes. Thus they were a channel of intellectual communication with the continent. Moreover their intellectual standards were high; so that when Joseph Butler, the future Bishop of Durham and one of the glories of English philosophy, proceeded from the Dissenting Academy at Tewkesbury to Oriel College, Oxford, he was struck by the inferiority of the Oxford standards; and complained of the waste of time on frivolous matters of disputation there, which profited him nothing. Nor was Butler the only distinguished alumnus of the academies. Thomas Secker, a future Archbishop of Canterbury, and Josiah Hort, an Irish archbishop, owed their grounding to Dissenting Academies; as did Daniel Defoe, Samuel Wesley, Isaac Watts, Daniel Neal, and two Tory high church politicians, Robert Harley, Earl of Oxford, and Henry St. John, Viscount Bolingbroke. Amongst famous teachers in these schools were numbered Charles Morton, afterwards Vice-President of Harvard University, Theophilus Gale, and Philip Doddridge, whose academy at Northampton attained an outstanding renown. Their contribution to English education, in letters and science, no less than theology, was one of the most noteworthy features of the century following the Restoration.

At the other, and lowest, end of the scale, this period witnessed also the phenomenal rise and expansion of the Charity School Movement, an immediate and most practical outcome of the doctrine of divine benevolence. The aim of these Charity Schools was severely utilitarian, and their curriculum simple. They were designed to provide an elementary instruction for the children of the poor, in order to enable them to read the Bible, and the improving literature published by the Society for Promoting Christian Knowledge (founded in 1698); so that reading, writing, and casting accounts comprised the whole of their curriculum. The poor boys and girls who received this education were not intended to proceed to grammar schools for further instruction; they were to be apprenticed after the completion of their course; and the Charity School education was designed not to raise them above their lowly social station. The number of these schools ran into thousands; and their importance lay in the twin circumstances that they provided an elementary instruction for the poorest children and that they were largely financed by the middle-class subscribers, who gave voluntary annual subscriptions. The schools represented an early experiment in local enterprise. It is a far cry indeed from the Charity School of the eighteenth century to the Forster Education Act of 1870; not to say the Butler Act of 1944. It is easy to pour scorn on the limited objectives, the narrow curriculum, the patronizing nature, and the comparatively small fraction of the population served by these Charity Schools. But the fact remains that the private benevolence, and Christian philanthropy of the late seventeenth and early eighteenth centuries, anticipated by more than a century and a half the acceptance by the State of the duty and responsibility of providing a primary education for its citizens.

But the most remarkable example of the practical application of the belief in the duty of benevolence was the hospital foundations of the age. In London no fewer than twelve hospitals, including some of the most famous, owed their establishment to this impulse: the Foundling, Guy's, St. George's, the Westminster, the London, the Middlesex; and half a dozen maternity hospitals. Generally throughout the country, the foundation of County Hospitals attested the same spirit of philanthropy; and in the two university towns, the Radcliffe and Addenbrooke's hospitals belong to this period. Few centuries could point to a more noteworthy achievement than these hospital foundations of the first three-quarters of the eighteenth century in particular. Indeed the support of hospitals by voluntary contributions became one of the popular exercises of the age. When a country clergyman of Norfolk, James Woodforde, whose voluminous diaries have won for him an entirely unexpected posthumous fame to-day, recorded in his pages periodic visits to Norwich cathedral, to attend performances of Handel's music, and to hear charity sermons on behalf of the public hospital, he was typical of the times in which he lived.

This age was by no means one of the ages of faith; but few epochs have given more convincing proof of their faith by works. If its favourite text was that upon which Archbishop Tillotson preached one of his best-known sermons—a sermon incidentally which was plagiarized and repeated in parish churches throughout the country— 'And His commandments are not grievous', it could plead in extenuation that charity covers a multitude of sins. Indeed in providing the rudiments of elementary education for social classes which otherwise would have been left wholly illiterate, and in establishing hospitals for the sick, and particularly for women in childbirth, it was mindful of the blessing bestowed upon the Good Samaritan, and on all who gave a cup of cold water to the little ones. Perhaps in so acting it was covetous of the reward promised to such good offices; but at least it had no illusion that faith without works was profitable to salvation.

15. DEISM AND DECLINE

'It is come, I know not how, to be taken for granted by many persons,' wrote Joseph Butler in 1736 in his *Analogy of Religion*, 'that Christianity is not so much as a subject of inquiry; but that it is now at length discovered to be fictitious; And accordingly they treat it as if, in the present age, this were an agreed point among all people of discernment.' The surprise of Bishop Butler may be shared at first sight by ourselves who may likewise ask, what had happened to the confident optimism of Locke and the scientists in the confirmation of the essential truths of Christianity by scientific discoveries, and in the concurrence of natural and revealed religion? It is true that the defenders of revelation had laboured somewhat heavily to establish that Christianity was a replication of natural religion, with additional authority and penal sanctions; and also that the champions of natural religion had removed a good many of the dogmatic outworks hitherto thought impregnable by orthodox theologians. But perhaps the chief factor in the change noted by Butler, had been the direct assault of the Deists upon even Locke's reduced minimum of Christian belief.

If the single article of the new creed was to be that Jesus was the Messiah whose advent was foretold by prophecy and the authenticity of whose mission was attested by miracles, then it became evidently necessary to establish beyond doubt the reality of predictive prophecy and the fact of miracles. Anthony Collins argued that the literal fulfilment of prophecies could not be maintained, and that allegorical or typical interpretation must suffice: 'It is most apparent,' he urged, 'that the whole gospel is in every respect founded on type and allegory; and that the apostles in most, if not in all cases, reasoned typically and allegorically.' On the other hand Thomas Woolston applied this allegorical method to the miracles recorded in the New Testament generally; and in particular to the crucial miracle of the resurrection of Christ. This he undertook to prove to be a 'monstrous and incredible miracle', and 'the most barefaced imposture that ever was put upon the world'; and concluded that the only escape was to accept a 'mystical interpretation of the whole story'. Already John Toland, a former Presbyterian exhibitioner at the university of Leyden, had argued that the mysteries of Christianity were due to the infiltration of pagan ideas, and that revelation could not embrace truths in themselves beyond the compass of reason. But the attack on prophecy and miracle was a direct laying of the axe to the root of the tree. In reply, orthodox divines began their laborious compilation of what Dr. Johnson aptly described as 'that Old Bailey theology, in which the apostles are being tried once a week for the capital crime of forgery'. Typical of this apologetic were the sermons of Thomas Sherlock, Master of the Temple, who treated his legal auditors to a protracted cross-examination of the apostles by judge, counsel, and jury for their testimony to the resurrection. His conclusion, quaintly stated, was in the form of a legal verdict. 'Judge: What say you, Are the Apostles guilty of giving false evidence in the case of the resurrection of Jesus, or not guilty? Foreman of the jury: Not guilty.'

The importance of this frontal assault on the fundamental articles of Christian belief was very considerable. It marked the onslaught of rationalistic criticism on the Bible; and it has been called with justice 'the beginning of modernity in English theology'. The Deists asked the right questions, even if they could not find the right answers. If in the course of their criticism, they hit upon some of the agreed conclusions of the Higher Critics of the nineteenth century, this was by chance rather than by scientific research. In particular they lacked one key to the unlocking of many doors, the concept of evolution as applied to religion and resulting in the theory of a development of doctrine. But it is indisputable that they raised some of the questions which fell to the lot of Biblical criticism a century and a half later to answer.

Some of the consequences of their speculations, however, were alarming for their age. Many would-be defenders of orthodoxy were desirous that the essential doctrines of Christianity should be stated only in Biblical terms and language; and that the elaborate definitions of the Nicene Creed and of the general councils should be avoided. Study of the New Testament led to a widespread and influential revival of Arian views of the person and status of Christ; and the Arianisers of the eighteenth century, like their prototypes of the fourth, claimed to be conservative Bible Christians, seeking to purify the primitive deposit of faith from pagan adulteration. In particular the English Presbyterians suffered a veritable landslide from orthodoxy into what later became known as Unitarianism. Arising from the Salters Hall controversy, the tendency spread; and the result was seriously to weaken and to disturb the proportions of Protestant Dissent, of which the Presbyterians had been the most numerous and weighty part. Within the established Church also the leaven exercised much influence. It was significant, for example, that Dr. Samuel Clarke, whose fame had been established by his Boyle lectures on the *Being and Attributes of God*, should proceed in his *Scripture Doctrine of the Trinity* to defend Arian conceptions of the Deity. Later in the century Richard Watson, Regius Professor of Divinity at Cambridge and afterwards Bishop of Llandaff, defended Unitarianism as essentially Christian, objected to the Athanasian doctrine of the Trinity 'because we cannot find it is literally contained in any passage of Holy Writ, or can by sound criticism be deduced from it'; and advocated a reform of Articles and Prayer Book in consonance with these ideas. For the movement was concerned with worship and liturgy no less than theology and found expression in revised forms of public worship, some of which were as revolutionary as adventurous.

At the same time the eighteenth century witnessed a marked decline of the religious fervour of its predecessor amongst all Churches. With the accession of the house of Hanover, an age of moderation, sobriety and convention began. The established Church was safeguarded by the Test and Corporation acts; and the Protestant Dissenters, secure in their toleration and much divided by theological controversies, settled down to a position of passive acquiescence. Politically their organization into the Dissenting Deputies enabled them to preserve the *status quo* as regards legal toleration, but not to extend it; and their acceptance of the royal bounty, the *regium donum*, as an annual contribution to their charities, signified their settling down to be at ease in Sion. To a considerable degree, the lethargy both of the establishment and of the Protestant Dissenters has been exaggerated and even caricatured, in order to bring out more brightly the Methodist revival. An age which numbered Isaac Watts and Philip Doddridge amongst Dissenters cannot be accused of lack of piety, hymnody, pastoral zeal, or theological learning; nor can the names of Butler, Gibson, Wake, and Secker in the established Church be considered synonymous with lethargy and worldliness. But a temper of pessimism had replaced the earlier optimism; and even Butler's refutation of the Deists in his *Analogy of Religion, Natural and Revealed*, helped in some ways to accentuate the gloom. For his masterly undermining of the Deist position by showing the existence of mysteries and dark corners in nature, and therefore among the actions of the God of nature, led to the conclusion that the ways of God to man can be justified only upon the basis of a future state of rewards and punishments, in which the evils and injustices of this world will be triumphantly redressed. But the mass of the people had as little understanding of as interest in these theological disputations. Moreover, the general standards of moral conduct were undoubtedly declining; and in a desperate struggle to improve the tone of society and of its citizens, a rationalistic creed, whether orthodox or deist, was impotent to arouse the emotions and effect conversion. For the renaissance of society, especially in prospect of the industrial and agricultural changes about to take place, there was urgent need of a revival of religion. It was the singular fortune of the English religious tradition that the hour and the men were matched in the person of John Wesley and his co-operators in the Methodist movements, of which I shall speak in my next two talks.

16. JOHN WESLEY AND THE METHODIST REVIVAL

'In the evening,' wrote John Wesley in his *Journal* of 24 May, 1738, 'I went very unwillingly to a society in Aldersgate street, where one was reading Luther's preface to the *Epistle to the Romans*. About a quarter before nine, while he was describing the change which God works in the heart through faith in Christ, I felt my heart strangely warmed. I felt I did trust in Christ, in Christ alone, for my salvation. And an assurance was given me that He had taken away my sins, even mine, and saved me from the law of sin and death.' Only three days before, Charles Wesley had experienced a similar conversion through Luther's Commentary on the *Epistle to the Galatians* (which, it is interesting to recall, had also been instrumental in the conversion of John Bunyan). From this experience of John Wesley, there issued a recall to religion, whose history is writ large on the face of the United Kingdom and the United States of America; and whose importance was reckoned by the historian, Lecky, higher than the victories of Chatham. It was indeed a turning point in evangelical religion among English-speaking peoples.

Not indeed that John Wesley had been converted from a life of impiety and ungodliness. Much the reverse; for he had been for ten years a priest of the Church of England, and the leader in Oxford of a high church movement, sacramental in emphasis and rigid in churchmanship, which might have developed into an eighteenth century anticipation of the Tractarian Movement. Moreover, he had visited North America as an apostle of this tradition, during which time he had been much influenced by certain Moravian Brethren in whose company he had crossed the Atlantic. His religious history indeed was woven of many strands. Both his grandfathers had been ejected from their livings in 1662; his father had been educated at a Dissenting Academy and afterwards had become a high churchman; and his mother before marriage had been latitudinarian with a tinge of the fashionable Socinianism. Similarly his own spiritual development owed much to the non-juror William Law and to the Moravian Peter Böhler. His conversion therefore was from the search for salvation by works to the assurance of salvation by faith. 'By a Christian I mean one who so believes in Christ that sin had no more dominion over him; and in this sense of the word I was not a Christian till May 24th.' The fruits of his conversion were seen in an evangelistic and pastoral ministry, lasting forty years, and involving his travelling on horseback between four and five thousand miles a year, and preaching an almost incredible number of sermons. The power of his conversion was such as to compel him to proclaim everywhere the good tidings of justification, assurance of salvation and forgiveness of sins, and sanctification with the consequent possibility of Christian perfection. 'I look upon all the world as my parish; thus far I mean, that in whatever part of it I am, I judge it meet, right, and my bounden duty, to declare unto all that are willing to hear, the glad tidings of salvation.' He preached to phenomenal numbers and in unaccustomed places; but throughout his long ministry he sought to avoid theological controversy, and to kindle all true religion of the heart into a living flame. 'Of Calvinism, Mysticism, and Antinomianism, have a care,' he wrote, 'for they are the bane of true religion; and one or other of them has been the grand hindrance of the work of God, wherever it has broken out.'

But his greatest quality lay in his unusual combination of gifts. 'In John Wesley,' observed B. L. Manning, 'the Methodists had a leader who, by a stroke of divine genius that puts him into the same rank as Hildebrand, St. Dominic, and St. Ignatius Loyola, combined the evangelical passion and experience of Luther with Calvin's ecclesiastical system.' He knew how easily religious zeal evaporated unless directed into right channels. Therefore, perhaps his supremely important talent was that of organization. By means of his Class System, binding his converts together both for mutual spiritual edification and for the exercise of philanthropy, he ensured the permanence of his work. As his local Societies grew, he expanded his organization into a nation-wide system, with the Annual Conference at the apex and the Class Meeting as the basis. By means of his preaching also, the Methodist revival turned the flank of the Deist and Arian controversies; for sinners convinced of the fact of sin and the reality of redemption, wasted no time in abstract theorizing about the precise definition of the Deity of the Christ who had saved them. Perhaps this was the most important immediate influence of Wesley on the religion of his age. 'We are not to fight against notions, but against sins.' But in driving sins out of the door, a good many notions fled also out of the window.

The second great achievement of Wesley was to bring the good news of the gospel to multitudes who had fallen outside the effective ministry of the existing churches, particularly the established Church. The Church of England indeed was hamstrung in face of the social changes consequent upon the industrial revolution; for a special act of parliament was necessary for the creation of each new parish; and thereby the establishment was fatally hampered in ministering to the aggregations of people gathered in new towns. To these, and to other social groups untouched by existing churches, Wesley was able to bring both a religious experience, and an organization which bound them to service in his societies. The discovery also of incandescent gas as a means of illumination was instrumental in enabling him to introduce the immensely successful experiment of Sunday evening services during autumn and winter.

For such a task of evangelism and organization, there was evident need of many helpers. Some of his lieutenants indeed were men of ability second only to his own, notably his brother Charles, George Whitefield, and Fletcher of Madeley. But the number of ordained ministers of the established Church who followed him, was sorely disappointing and insufficient. Therefore he had to fall back on the services of lay preachers, an institution which led to increasing difficulties with the bishops of the Church of England, who would not admit them to holy orders. Moreover Wesley, in accordance with his own sacramental doctrine, sought to train his converts to regular and frequent reception of the Holy Communion. As his work expanded, it was natural that Methodists should desire to receive the Lord's Supper at the hands of their own preachers, from whose lips they heard the Word of God. This growing demand was probably the most potent factor making for separation from the Church of England. In time, Wesley himself was driven to ordain ministers, at first for North America, then for Scotland, and finally for England, in order to meet this need. It should be recognized, however, that in taking this step he was only acting on his settled conviction of more than a generation, of the identity of the New Testament bishop and presbyter. Since 1746 he had been convinced that he had 'as good a right to ordain as to administer the Lord's Supper', because 'bishops and presbyters are the same order, and consequently have the same right to ordain'. His long, self-denying ordinance in not exercising this right was solely due to his desire 'not to violate the established order of the national church'. His action, however, laid the foundation for the Methodist Episcopal Church in the United States, as well as leading to the formal separation, after his death, of the Methodist Societies from the established Church at home. Moreover, the Methodists were shortly to step into the place of the Presbyterians as the largest body of Protestants outside the Church of England; and in modern reunion discussions they take a prominent place as being still nearest to that Church of all English Free Churches.

To the Methodist revival also English-speaking Christianity owes a hymnody to which all Protestant churches stand deeply indebted. Charles Wesley was pre-eminently the poet and hymnodist of the movement; and his hymns did as much, if not more, than the sermons of his brother to popularize the Arminian doctrine that Christ died for all and that God willeth all men to come to a knowledge of salvation. Just as the Lutheran reformation had produced a wealth of German hymns, and its Calvinist counterpart the famous Metrical Psalter, so the Methodist revival enriched English Christianity with a hitherto unequalled volume of spiritual hymns and songs. Historians have long recognized the providential concurrence of Methodism and the social revolution wrought by the industrial changes of the eighteenth century; and history may be claimed to have confirmed fully John Wesley's own verdict on his work: 'We came neither too soon, nor too late. Our Lord's time is the best time.'

17. THE EVANGELICAL REVIVAL IN THE CHURCH OF ENGLAND

'Whenever I go to Oxford,' wrote George Whitefield shortly before his death, 'I cannot help running to the spot where Jesus Christ first revealed himself to me, and gave me the new birth. I learned that a man may go to church, say his prayers, receive the sacrament, and yet not be a Christian. . . . I discovered that they who know anything of religion, know it is a vital union with the Son of God—Christ formed in the heart. O, what a ray of divine life did then break in upon my soul!' Three years before the conversion of John Wesley, his colleague in the Evangelical revival of their century, George Whitefield had experienced a similar awakening at the age of sixteen. It is difficult to think of the one without the other; for they ran both together in the early stages of Methodism; and at first indeed Whitefield outran Wesley. He was undoubtedly the greater orator, drawing to his sermons not only humble manual workers, but members of the upper social classes, including not only devout ladies like his patroness Selina, Countess of Huntingdon, but also the worldly-wise Lord Chesterfield and the sceptical philosopher, David Hume. He was also bolder in pioneering, being the first to essay the experiment of field preaching, to employ lay preachers, to visit North America, and to establish or encourage new educational foundations both in this country and the new world. As a preacher, he was the fiery torch of the revival, but he lacked the organizing genius of Wesley; and the Countess of Huntingdon's Connexion, which was the visible expression of his labours, was small compared with Wesley's Methodist societies. Moreover, the two leaders were divided deeply by that rift which had so often split the forces of Protestantism, the controversy of Calvinist versus Arminian. Whitefield was a rigid Calvinist; and though he and Wesley agreed amicably to differ on the matters at issue between themselves, they realized that continued co-operation was impossible. Their followers unfortunately failed to imitate this charity; and one of the most painful episodes in English religious history is the bitter controversy between Calvinist and Arminian amongst the *epigoni* of their disciples.

Historically, moreover, the Evangelical Revival within the Church of England was an offshoot from the Calvinist movement of Whitefield. Indeed one of the great disappointments of John Wesley's later years was to find himself excluded from the pulpits of the 'awakened' Anglican clergy on the ground of his Arminianism. At first the common profession of Calvinism overrode denominational differences. Sheltering behind the protective influence of the Countess of Huntingdon, the theological college founded at Trevecca in 1768, trained ministers indifferently for episcopal and non-episcopal churches. The London Missionary Society was deliberately undenominational in character; whilst the British and Foreign Bible Society had a dual secretariat of an Anglican and a Dissenting minister. Other evidences of this co-operation were perhaps more anomalous; as when Anglican incumbents, such as Grimshaw at Haworth and Venn at Huddersfield, subscribed towards the building of independent chapels within Anglican parishes, in order to maintain the continuity of Calvinist preaching when a change of parish minister threatened deviations. Similarly, Grimshaw and Berridge borrowed from Whitefield the practice of itinerancy, by which they exercised the freedom to invade other parishes than their own for the purpose of spreading their evangel. A sharp blow indeed was directed against this co-operation, when in 1780 several chapels founded under the ægis of the Countess of Huntingdon, took out licences as Dissenting chapels, and when in 1783 some of her chaplains assumed the authority to ordain. Thus the parting of the ways was reached between the Anglican Evangelicals and the Calvinistic Methodists, and the former readjusted their relations alike with the former allies and with their fellow-churchmen.

Perhaps the most influential and important leader of the newer generation of Anglican Evangelicals was Charles Simeon, whose long ministry in Cambridge marked a turning point in the religious history of both town and university. At first Simeon himself had indulged in an itinerant ministry; but his later abandonment of this practice and his discouragement of it in others, diverted the Evangelical movement into more fruitful parochial channels, and thereby domesticated it firmly within the established Church. Even more important was his leadership in the foundation of the Church Missionary Society, by means of which Anglican Evangelicals were able to support their own missionary activity and to withdraw from association with Dissenters in the London Missionary Society. For such actions Simeon earned from opponents the reproach of being 'more of a Church-man than a Gospel-man'; but his strategy enabled his followers to make a distinctive and recognized contribution to their own Church. Accordingly the Church of England was renewed by its own version of the eighteenth century revival; and when the turn of the century arrived, the most active element within its ranks was the Evangelical school of churchmanship. Their primary emphasis lay upon the need for personal conversion and individual experience of forgiveness and justification by faith. If in one aspect they appeared to share the latitudinarian persuasion 'that if we should be shut out of heaven for our sins, it will be no great comfort to us what church we were members of on earth'; on another side it should be remembered that they provided a good deal of the driving force of the new missionary expansion of the Church, and a not inconsiderable element of the personnel of the Anglican episcopates set up in India, Canada and Australasia. There was perhaps more than a grain of truth mingled with a coating of malice in the observation that, whilst the leaders of the Tractarian movement were thundering forth the theoretical necessity of bishops to a Church, the Evangelicals were sending out bishops to various parts of what was to become the second British Empire.

But perhaps the most remarkable influence of the revival was upon the religious and social life of the Church in England. Its missionary and philanthropic enterprises indeed are sufficiently important to receive separate mention. Within the established Church itself, a new spirit was kindled and new standards of pastoral duty attained. The long ministry of Simeon at Holy Trinity Church, Cambridge, became a model of evangelical parochial duty. Moreover he essayed a new solution to the problem of continuity of teaching and churchmanship, which indeed brought its own problems for future generations. Older Evangelicals like Grimshaw, Berridge and Venn, had sought to ensure this continuity, as has been remarked, by the foundation of independent chapels within existing parishes, in which episcopally ordained ministers would officiate, the Book of Common Prayer be used, and Calvinistic doctrine be preached. But the weaknesses of this expedient lay in the setting-up, if not of altar against altar, yet of pulpit against pulpit; and in the practical circumstance that in the second generation these chapels lost their affiliation to the established Church, and became formally Dissenting chapels. Instead, Simeon devoted a portion of his wealth to the purchase of advowsons, by which present provision might be made in face of episcopal hostility for Evangelical clergy to minister, and a better guarantee of future continuity be furnished. Thus Simeon's Trustees inaugurated the history of ecclesiastical party trusts. The measure was an obvious improvement on earlier methods; but it produced a crop of difficulties, when imitated, for future generations. A pronounced weakness of the Evangelical school was its general indifference to scholarship and learning, though many of its leaders were themselves academic scholars; and what would now be called its Fundamentalist attitude towards the Bible. But its services to the Church of England by the revival of personal and individual religion were great, alike in its own generation and in prospect of the revolutionary changes to come in the Victorian age.

18. THE SOCIAL CONSCIENCE: SLAVERY, FACTORIES, MINES, AND EDUCATION

'UNLESS the Divine Power has raised you up to be an *Athanasius contra mundum*, I do not see how you can go through your glorious enterprise,' wrote John Wesley to William Wilberforce on 24th February, 1791. 'Go on in the name of God and in the power of his might, till even American slavery (the vilest that ever saw the sun) shall vanish away before it.' The letter was endorsed by its recipient 'John Wesley; his last words; slave trade.' Within a week of writing it, Wesley had died; and his last written exhortation therefore was to one of the leading Evangelical laymen of the Church of England to persevere in a crusade which is the best known expression of the nascent social conscience of the churches. For the slave trade was as lucrative as long-established; and a demand for its total abolition, based solely upon religious and ethical considerations, was a new phenomenon. The Quakers had long been honourably distinguished by their zeal in this cause and now they were joined by representatives of other Churches. Indeed the peculiar glory of the campaign was that it was led by Christian laymen. The influence of the Clapham Sect was one of the distinguishing features of the Anglican Evangelical revival; for it numbered such men of social position as Wilberforce, Henry and Robert Thornton, Granville Sharp, Zachary Macaulay, James Stephen, Charles Grant, and Lord Teignmouth. In the House of Commons the cause was supported by prominent Nonconformists, such as Thomas Thompson, William Smith and Joseph Butterworth. Their first success was gained in 1807, when Charles James Fox shed a transient lustre on his ministerial office by carrying a bill for the abolition of slavery in British possessions; and their final victory was in 1833, when the emancipation of slaves was effected at a cost of £20,000,000 to the British taxpayer. Both Wellington and Castlereagh recognized this not only as a remarkable achievement in itself, but as presaging the growth of a Christian social conscience.

There was evident need of such a factor in the national life; for the social results of the industrial revolution were grave and formidable. Thanks in part to the aggravation of war, and in part also to the prevailing political philosophy of *laisser-faire*, no attempt had been made by Parliament to legislate for the health and welfare, both in factories and in their homes, of the manual operatives who had crowded into the new industrial towns. The inventive genius of science as applied to industry had outrun the moral capacity of man, just as in the present age a similar application of science to destructive engines of war threatens to extinguish mankind unless controlled. The legacy of a quarter of a century of war against France was that a virtual moratorium had been imposed on all socially ameliorative measures. Hence there was urgent need to break down the *laisser-faire* principle, and to assert the right of Parliament to concern itself with what came shortly to be known as 'the condition-of-the people' question. The leader of the campaign for limitation of hours of work in factories and mines was another Anglican Evangelical layman, Lord Shaftesbury. In 1833 a government bill was passed to forbid the employment in industry of children under nine years of age; to limit the hours of work for young people between nine and eighteen years, to fix a maximum working-day of twelve hours and of sixty-nine hours a week, and to provide for the compulsory right of entry into factories of four full-time salaried state-inspectors. In 1842 a Mines Act was passed to exclude women and girls from underground work in mines, to fix the minimum age for the employment of boys at ten years of age, and again to provide for the official inspection of mines. Finally, in 1844, a new Factory Act codified earlier legislation, and in 1846 another Act was carried establishing the ten-hour working day. It is a far cry indeed from these tentative steps to the modern Welfare State and five-day and forty-hour working week. But these initial reforms not only established much-needed limitations on industrial employment, but asserted the principle of state intervention in the interests of the health and welfare of its citizens. As the first-fruits of the growth of a Christian social conscience, they were equally important and significant; though indeed here also they were but the first-fruits of a movement, which, during the nineteenth century, was to seek increasingly to apply religion to the problems of society and the state.

The same year, 1833, which saw the emancipation of slaves, witnessed also the first government grant of £20,000 in support of voluntary primary schools. The pioneer work of the churches in popular education has been already mentioned in connection with the Charity School Movement. Methodism had given a great impetus to education, both Wesley and Whitefield having been zealous in their efforts to provide religious education for the poor. An Anglican layman Robert Raikes and a lay-woman Hannah Moore had tried to improve the status of manual workers by setting up Sunday Schools, which, though restricted both in hours of assembly and by the limitations of instructors, at least taught their pupils to read. With the increasing demands of industry on youth, however, opportunities for education were obviously severely limited. Two pioneers in the foundation of Day Schools in the early nineteenth century were the Quaker, Joseph Lancaster, and an Anglican clergyman, Andrew Bell; each of whom, experimenting independently, hit upon the expedient of the monitorial system. From the former there sprang the British and Foreign Schools Society; and from the latter the National Society of the Church of England; and there ensued a vigorous, if not always friendly, rivalry between the two societies to plan Day Schools throughout the country. The bone of contention was the undenominational or denominational character of the religious teaching to be given; and when the government grant of 1833 was allotted, the greater part went to the National Schools because of their greater financial support in the country. In 1840 an Education Committee of the Privy Council was formed, and an additional £10,000 voted for popular education; and the first 'Normal College' for the training of teachers founded. Thus there came into existence the divergence between Anglicans and Nonconformists concerning the management, staffing, and religious instruction of these schools. When in 1870 by the Forster Education Act, the State for the first time accepted responsibility for the provision of primary education for all children, it accepted also the *status quo* in two important respects; by allowing the co-existence of church schools and board schools, and by providing for undenominational religious teaching only in the board schools, with a conscience clause allowing parents to withdraw their children from such instruction.

This act inaugurated more than half a century of acute controversy between the Churches concerning popular education; in which the Anglicans contended for the principle of denominational schools and the Nonconformists against it. The disputes were as melancholy as protracted, leading to the passive resistance of prominent Freechurchmen, such as Dr. John Clifford, after the Balfour Education Act of 1902 had thrown denominational schools on the public rates, thereby compelling Nonconformists to contribute to the maintenance of church schools. The conflict was productive of much friction; and not until the Butler Education Act of 1944 was this sombre chapter brought to a conclusion. The inter-Church education controversies of the nineteenth century belong now (it may be hoped) to the category of 'far-off, forgotten things, and battles long ago'. For the Butler Act provided for religious teaching and acts of worship as an integral part of primary and secondary education; and the era of Agreed Syllabuses for such teaching has replaced that of struggle for or against the introduction of religious instruction in state-controlled schools. Few of the ecclesiastical conflicts of the last century have enjoyed such a happy ending as those raging round popular education. In few fields has the spirit of Christian unity and co-operation achieved such a far-reaching and important victory over divisive denominational differences.

19. THE AGE OF REFORM

'THE Church as it now stands,' wrote Thomas Arnold in 1832, 'no human power can save.' 'The Church of England,' rejoiced his contemporary Jeremy Bentham, 'is ripe for dissolution.' Neither anticipation seemed too gloomy in the fever of reform which characterized the 1830's. The long moratorium imposed by war was over; and eager hands were stretching out, not to steady but to overturn the ark of the Covenant. In 1828 the symbols of Anglican exclusiveness, the Test and Corporation Acts, were at length repealed; and if their disappearance from the statute book, like the fall of the Bastille commemorated in French history, was rather the demolition of a dismantled fortress than the storming of a present redoubt, it was none the less a landmark. In the following year Roman Catholic Emancipation was carried; and the floodgates seemed open to the enemies of the established Church, alike Protestant and Papist, to sweep away its position. Jeremy Bentham, in accordance with the principles of Utilitarianism, was indeed meantime perfecting his scheme for the disendowment of the Church of England, and the diversion of its revenues to the foundation of a National Mechanics' Institute. In 1828 there had been founded also University College, London, the first institution of university status in England to avow a purely secular basis for its education. Alike in Parliament, in municipal corporations, in the penal and judicial system, and in the established Church, the demand for reform was heard; and the unanswered question was whether revolution might not follow so swiftly upon the heels of reform as to outpace the champions of moderate reconstruction.

It was undeniable that the established Church stood in urgent need of drastic reform. Apart from its repudiation of the papacy, the sixteenth century Reformation had been primarily doctrinal and liturgical; whilst the financial and administrative system had been substantially unchanged. Hoary medieval abuses, such as plurality, non-residence, inequalities of income, and sinecures, had been aggravated by the changing value of land, as a result of the industrial revolution. Thanks to the Ecclesiastical Commission appointed by Sir Robert Peel, and the carrying out of its recommendations by his Whig successors, the revenues of bishoprics were brought nearer to equality, the endowments of simple prebends in cathedrals confiscated; and the surplus revenues thus acquired were devoted to the creation of new dioceses in the industrial north, to the foundation of new parishes and the provision of stipends, and to the payment of curates. These reforms made possible the enforcement of residence and the prohibition of plurality. But, though the measures of reform were cumulatively thoroughgoing, they did not approach disendowment; and their smooth operation was the means of enabling the established Church to adapt itself to the needs and conditions of a new age; and to make up the leeway of the industrial revolution. Without them it is difficult to conceive how the ideals of pastoral work, propagated by the leaders of the Oxford Movement, could have been put into practice. As a result of their enforcement, what friends of the Church had feared and foes desired, its dissolution, was once again postponed, despite all appearances to the contrary.

For the Protestant Dissenters, the repeal of the Test and Corporation Acts was but the prelude to a sustained campaign for complete equality. Many restrictions upon them still continued, such as the compulsory payment of church rates, and the necessity to have recourse to the parish church for marriages and burials. The struggle to throw off these vestiges of inequality was long and embittered; and thanks to the resistance of the established Church, did much to infect ecclesiastical relationships with a spirit of malice and envy. Moreover, the two ancient universities of Oxford and Cambridge were opened only gradually to non-Anglicans. An immediate result of this hostility was the creation of the Liberation Society, to encompass the disestablishment and disendowment of the Anglican Church. In 1869 this succeeded in Ireland; but no further victory was achieved until the disestablishment of the Church in Wales was carried at the outbreak of the first German war of the present century. In England the agitation for disestablishment has now almost disappeared; and this is not the only evidence of the emergence of happier and more cordial relationships between the Church of England and the Free Churches.

In order to meet the manifold challenge of the new situation, the Nonconformist Churches also drew closer together; at first by the foundation of the Congregational and Baptist Unions in 1831, and in the present century by the emergence in 1919 of the Free Church Federal Council. But the balance of power within Nonconformity had been profoundly altered by the results, on the one hand of the landslide of English Presbyterians into Unitarianism, and on the other of the establishment of the Wesleyan Methodist Church. Unfortunately, the first half of the nineteenth century witnessed a serious weakening of the Methodists by a series of melancholy controversies and secessions. In part these were due to the distaste shown by a more conventional and conservative generation of Methodists for the recurrence of the phenomena of 'enthusiasm', familiar to their grandparents; but in greater part they represented the emergence of a democratic element which demanded an end of the system of government bequeathed by John Wesley. He indeed had ruled his Societies autocratically, conscious of his superior education and status compared with the great majority of his fellow-workers. Moreover he had transmitted his authority to the Legal Hundred, composed of ministers chosen by himself and empowered to fill by co-option vacancies caused by death. Soon there developed an increasing revolt, both of ministers against the unrepresentative and irresponsible Legal Hundred, and of laymen against its exclusively clerical composition. During the hegemony of Jabez Bunting, who wielded a quasi-pontifical influence in Methodism, conflict became exacerbated; and after the painful Fly-Sheet controversy of the middle 1840's, secessions and expulsions on a considerable scale ensued. Soon a United Methodist Free Church stood over against the parent body; and not until 1877 did the Wesleyan Methodist Church admit laymen to its Annual Conference; whilst the full reunion of Methodists was not achieved until 1932. But if these quarrels and secessions weakened the corporate influence of Methodism, they had compensating advantages; for the assertion of democratic principles by the radical Methodists ensured that contemporary radical movement in politics, notably Chartism, should not lack religious sympathizers and supporters. From the Methodist secessions there developed leaders of left-wing social movements; thanks to which English political Radicalism and Socialism have been saved from anti-clerical and anti-Christian bias.

But it was in the field of theological education that the nineteenth century witnessed the most promising advances towards mutual understanding between the Nonconformist Churches and the Church of England. The University Tests Act of Gladstone, passed in 1871, threw open all offices in the ancient universities, except clerical fellowships, headships of houses and divinity professorships, to non-Anglicans. In 1879 Robert F. Horton, who had entered New College, Oxford, in 1874, was elected to a fellowship. Perhaps the most important consequence of the changes was the migration of Free Church theological colleges to the universities. At Oxford the way was led by the Congregationalist Mansfield College in 1889, followed by the Unitarian Manchester College in 1893, and by Regents' Park Baptist College in 1928. To Cambridge there came the Presbyterian Westminster College in 1899, Cheshunt College of the Countess of Huntingdon's Connexion in 1901, and Wesley House in 1921. Nor should the contribution of the Free Churches to the modern civic universities be overlooked; for the establishment in these cities of their several colleges prepared the way for the recent creation of theological faculties in several of the modern universities. In all these academic centres co-operation between Anglicans and Free Churchmen in teaching, examining, and administration is close and cordial. Indeed it was this *rapprochement* at the highest educational level which made possible the ideal and fulfilment of the Butler Education Act in the primary and secondary schools. In the field of education at least the English religious tradition has made evident how good and joyful it is for brethren to dwell together in unity.

20. THE OXFORD MOVEMENT

'WHEREVER I go about the country,' wrote Thomas Sikes to Dr. Pusey in 1833, 'I see amongst the clergy a number of very amiable and estimable men, many of them much in earnest, and wishing to do good. But I have observed one universal want in their teaching, the uniform suppression of one, great truth. There is no account given anywhere, so far as I can see, of the One, Holy Catholic Church. . . . We hear not a breath about the Church; bye and bye, those who live to see it, will hear of nothing else; and just in proportion perhaps to its present suppression will be its future development.' Rarely has predictive prophecy been more justified by events. Sikes had put his finger unerringly on the gap in Anglican teaching at the beginning of the Oxford Movement, and on the most important characteristic of the Tractarian tradition. In part of course the movement was a call to arms against the dangerous tendencies of the reform age. To Newman its primary objective, as declared in the first of the *Tracts for the Times*, was to arouse the clergy to a sense alike of their peril and of their supernatural commission. To Newman also, its further aim was to combat the insidious penetration of liberalism in Church, university, and nation. But the Tractarian movement was also a reaction against the predominance of the Evangelical school, and a revival of the seventeenth century High-church tradition. Not indeed that this school of churchmanship had been left wholly without witness during the long winter since the secession of the Non-jurors. The Clapton Sect, embracing influential laymen and clergymen, had continued to walk in the old paths; and John Keble had been reared in the principles of the Oxford Movement, before either movement or name were begun. But whereas they had been among the quiet in the land, the urgency of the spirit of reform which was threatening all traditional institutions, required now an active campaign instead of passive resistance.

It was natural that the new movement should centre in the person of a leader, and of those qualified for leadership, John Henry Newman was outstanding. A great deal of the first phase of the revival therefore was connected with the individual religious and theological development of Newman. Lacking the roots of Keble and Pusey in the historic High-church tradition, he moved with considerable rapidity from confidence to despair, from leadership to secession. His pristine assurance was marked. 'I had a supreme confidence in our cause; we were upholding that primitive Christianity which was delivered once for all by the early teachers of the Church, and which was registered and attested in the Anglican formularies and by the Anglican divines.' But a series of events—some of them historical, such as his studies of the ancient Donatist schism, and some contemporary, such as the Jerusalem Bishopric project—shook him profoundly; and forced him to reconsider whether the Church of England was in fact the Catholic Church of the realm. *Tract XC* represented his attempt to justify his position by an interpretation of the Thirty-Nine Articles as concordant with the Council of Trent; which R. W. Church thought 'far-fetched and artificial' in some instances. It was noteworthy, moreover, that the standard of Catholicity by which Newman measured the Articles was that of the Council of Trent rather than of the first five centuries of the Church. In 1845 there came the logical issue of this process in Newman's secession to Rome.

But the remarkable consequence of this shattering blow was that the Oxford Movement did not falter under the loss of its leader. Keble and Pusey set themselves to rally their followers; and the Movement first consolidated its position theologically, and then spread from the university into parishes throughout England, where the second generation of its disciples began a revolution in the ideals and outward accompaniments of public worship. Moreover, although personalities were of great influence on its history, the movement was more a matter of principles than of individual persons; and it is to these principles that the attention must be turned to assess its importance. As Sikes had foretold, by far the most influential of its tenets was its doctrine of the Church. Both in Keble's *Christian Year* and in the *Tracts for the Times* the new note struck was that of the authority of the Church and the duty of the individual to obey the Church. But for the Tractarians episcopacy was of the *esse* of the Church, and episcopal ordination necessary for a valid ministry and sacraments. 'We must necessarily consider none to be *really* ordained, who have not thus been ordained,' Newman wrote in the first of the Tracts. Moreover, the apostolic succession thus asserted was conceived, not as the maintenance of the chain of holders of the same bishop's throne, but as the connection between consecrated and consecrators from the apostles to the present bishops. It was evident that from such a standpoint the Jerusalem Bishopric scheme, which provided for a Protestant bishop, alternately of Lutheran and Anglican provenance, to shepherd the faithful of both Churches in the Holy Land, was anathema. It became clear also that the emphasis on apostolic succession drove a wedge between the Church of England and other Protestant Churches, both at home and abroad. In another field, the appeal to the primitive Church and to the first five centuries of its history, which continued as the basis of Tractarian defence against Rome, no less after than before Newman's secession, led to a great impetus for patristic study. An extensive series of translations of patristic works was published under the title of *The Library of the Fathers*; followed by a parallel series of the *Library of Anglo-Catholic Theology*.

It would be difficult to exaggerate the importance of these historical and theological studies.

Nor should it ever be forgotten that the movement was first and foremost a revival of religion. 'To such men,' R. W. Church observed of its leaders, 'religion really meant the most aweful and most seriously personal thing on earth'; and the most learned contemporary bishop, Connop Thirlwall, discerned that the movement was 'bent, with a deep consciousness and warm earnestness, upon high, practical ends'. In particular it stressed the note of holiness in churchmanship; and sought to train its disciples to a disciplined, orderly life of devotion and morality. Its ambition was not controversy but the training of saints; and to this end it turned to sacramental devotion, to fasting and other forms of asceticism, to auricular confession and spiritual direction, and to an emphasis upon clerical celibacy, and upon vocation both for women and men to the religious life. The second generation of its converts sought also to give expression to sacramental doctrine in ceremonial adjuncts; and the so-called ritual controversies which ensued were amongst the most deplorable episodes of the history of the movement and of the established Church.

The influence of the Oxford Movement upon the Church of England as a whole can scarcely be exaggerated. By its doctrine of the Church and of episcopacy it has altered profoundly the balance of the Anglican tradition; and in all modern discussions of ecclesiastical reunion it has forced episcopacy into the foreground. It has introduced new ideals of pastoral and priestly duty and restored patristic study. Perhaps its greatest influence however has been in the ordering of public worship. Few parish churches and cathedrals to-day have not felt the influence of its standards, especially in the restoration of a dignified ceremonial. At the same time it has brought many new and difficult problems for the Church of England, in the relationship of the several schools of churchmanship within its own communion and in its relations with other Churches, both Protestant and Roman Catholic. Probably the wisest verdict on its history is that of Mandell Creighton: 'Priesthood, sacraments, confession are all explicable by themselves. They can be placed in a system which finds room for individual liberty or in a system which excludes it. . . . The question to be decided is, How much of the results of the

Oxford Movement are to be permanently incorporated into the Anglican system? And the answer is, from my point of view: As much as is compatible with the maintenance of that system, as founded on a view of the Church which safeguards liberty.'

21. THE ROMAN CATHOLIC REVIVAL

In the autobiography of Bishop W. B. Ullathorne, whose long life spanned almost the entire nineteenth century, there is a moving and attractive picture of a Roman Catholic congregation at Scarborough in Yorkshire before the days of emancipation. They enjoyed the services of a priest every sixth Sunday only; and 'on the five intervening Sundays between the sacerdotal visits, it was arranged that the flock should attend chapel morning and afternoon as usual. First, the usual prayers before Mass were said aloud, then all in silence read the prayers for Mass in *The Garden of the Soul*, making a sort of spiritual communion, and then the lector for the week read one of Archer's sermons aloud. In the afternoon, the psalm prayers were chanted aloud; "All ye works of the Lord", etc.; and Catechism was heard.' The good bishop further added: 'As to Confirmation, no one of us children had ever seen a bishop.' The picture was typical of the scattered, isolated congregations, dependent for Mass and the Sacraments upon the occasional visit of a priest, during the eighteenth century. For even after the appointment in 1688 by Innocent XI of Four Vicars Apostolic for England, serving respectively the London, Midlands, Northern and Western districts, the bishop was still an itinerant and often fugitive figure, and the number of priests small. The mention in Ullathorne's memoirs of readings from *The Garden of the Soul* moreover, recalls one of the most heroic of the Vicars Apostolic, Richard Challenor, who for forty years strove to preserve his flock in fidelity to the Roman Catholic faith.

Challenor's long ministry indeed was an epitome of the history of his Church during the century before emancipation. His conception of the office and work of a bishop comprised not only the accepted episcopal functions of confirmation, ordination, visitation and the administration of ecclesiastical discipline, but also the provision of aids to faith and devotion in the shape of a translation of the Bible, meditations for individual piety, histories of British saints, and apologetic and polemical works of theology. His ministrations were conducted in the greatest secrecy for fear of detection; he was in journeyings oft, and in labours more abundant; he had the oversight also of his fellow-churchmen in the North American colonies; and he had to seek to reconcile and unite secular and regular clergy in face of many obstacles. He was sustained in his onerous office by a strong sense of duty, in which the fear of God as well as his love was prominent, and he represented the sober and restrained piety of the pre-ultramontane age. Like Moses, he lived to be within sight of the Promised Land.

With the grant of emancipation in 1829, the outward scene was swiftly changed; and it was little surprising if the traditional Roman Catholic gentry found much difficulty in adapting themselves to the new conditions and the new publicity. A community which, like Plato's men in the cave, had emerged for the first time for two and a half centuries as a Church into the full sunlight, rubbed its eyes with surprise and wonder. Other factors too contributed to a rapidity of advance in numbers and organization, which to conservative minds seemed too sudden to be lasting. Irish immigration during the first half of the nineteenth century was large; in 1841 the number of Irish immigrants totalled 224,128; only ten years later in 1851 it had risen to 419,256. This brought a great influx of Roman Catholic population into large industrial towns, particularly into seaport towns, and created the problem of a proletarian, urban flock sorely needing the provision of churches, priests, presbyteries and schools. From another source, so entirely different as hardly to seem to possess any common interest, the Oxford Movement, there came also a cohort of converts, comparatively small indeed in numbers, but exceedingly important and influential in personnel, as may be sufficiently seen from the names of Newman and Manning. The task of welding together these three diverse and almost contradictory elements, the traditional Roman Catholic landed families, the Irish immigrants, and the fastidious, academic converts from Anglicanism was sufficient to tax the wisdom and energy of the ablest prelates. Moreover, a new wind of doctrine was blowing into England from the European continent, that of Ultramontanism with its leanings to the opinion of Papal Infallibility, and its antipathy alike to the Gallicanism of the French Church and the timid fears of a too-forward policy entertained by the English Roman Catholics of pre-emancipation days.

It was the singular fortune of the Church of Rome to produce a series of active, energetic, and talented leaders to marshal these forces and to weld them into unity. First of these great figures was Nicholas Wiseman, who returned to England in 1840 as Vicar Apostolic, when Gregory XVI doubled their number in this country. Wiseman inaugurated and developed a vigorous theological and literary offensive, through lectures, books, and the newly-founded *Dublin Review*, and the more popular *Tablet*. After only a decade, in 1850 Pius IX resolved to restore a territorial Roman Catholic hierarchy in England instead of the apostolic vicariates; and Wiseman became first Archbishop of Westminster and Cardinal. His own inauguration of the new régime by means of a Pastoral Letter *Ex Porta Flaminia* provoked a considerable *émeute* in England, and a last outburst of anti-papal fury. Its speedy subsidence enabled the new bishops (of whom Ullathorne became Bishop of Birmingham) to devote their attention to the vast problems of ecclesiastical organization, of church-building, and of recruitment for the priesthood. The secession of Newman from Anglicanism in 1845 had signalized the beginning of a new era for Roman Catholicism amongst the educated classes of England; but that of Henry Edward Manning in 1851 was to revolutionize the position and influence of the Roman Catholic Church in this country. Ordained priest within ten weeks of his conversion, Manning within six years was appointed by Pius IX to be Provost of the Chapter of Westminster Cathedral; and in 1865 the same Pope nominated him as Wiseman's successor in the see of Westminster, and raised him to the cardinalate in 1875.

It would be almost impossible to overstate the importance of Manning's archiepiscopate to the Roman Catholic Church in England; for he is the founder of its modern position and influence. At the outset he realized the responsibility of providing for the religious and educational needs of the growing number of his fellow-churchmen. It was an act of particular boldness for him to adopt the maxim of 'schools before churches'; and thereby to concentrate his efforts primarily in the field of education. After the Forster Education Act of 1870, Manning inaugurated a campaign for Roman Catholic elementary schools, which eventually raised £350,000 to provide for 70,000 children. It was in this field that his educational work was most successful. In that of higher education his projects were not successful; and it has been left for his successors in the present century to bring Roman Catholics fully into the university life and studies of England. His knowledge of the social conditions of the Irish immigrants brought him also into the field of social reform; particularly into the achievement of national fame by his intervention and leading part in the settlement of the London Dockers' strike in 1889. From the same source sprang his advocacy of Irish Home Rule, and his connections with Gladstone and the Liberal Party in English politics. In the specifically religious field, Manning was a fervent Ultramontane, not only a staunch defender of the temporal power of the papacy, but still more a tireless protagonist for the definition at the Vatican Council in 1870 of Papal Infallibility. Perhaps his greatest achievement was his conversion of the English Roman Catholic community from its traditional conservatism to a fully-fledged Ultramontanism. Since his death others have built upon his foundations, and carried further his work; and at the present time the Roman Catholic Church plays a full part in the political, social, literary and intellectual life of the nation. Not the least remarkable virtue of the English religious tradition has been its capacity to absorb into the richness of its heritage the Roman Catholic renaissance of the last century and a quarter.

22. GOD AND CAESAR

'THEIR whole hierarchy or kingdom of darkness,' wrote Thomas Hobbes of the medieval Church, 'may be compared not unfitly to the "kingdom of fairies", that is to the old wives' fables in England concerning ghosts and spirits and the feats they play in the night.' If the seventeenth century State, whose apologia Hobbes penned, and whose apogee could be seen in the France of Louis XIV or in the military dictatorship of Oliver Cromwell in England, had so little difficulty in scattering this kingdom of fairies, how could the Church hope to withstand the national states of nineteenth and twentieth century Europe? For with the contagious example of the French Revolution as its pattern, the nineteenth century saw the rise of powerful national kingdoms, equipped with hitherto unprecedented means of moulding and influencing opinion and with still more formidable means of crushing opposition. Furthermore, these new states had not only the success of the French Revolution to encourage them, but also the earlier capitulation of the papacy to the Enlightened Despots of the eighteenth century, at whose behest it had consented to the suppression of the Jesuit order. *L'appétit vient en mangeant*; the modern nation-state was avid for power; and across its path stood the Christian Church, the traditional custodian of education, poor relief and other forms of social service, shortly to be undertaken by the civil power. How did the peculiar English tradition of the relations between Church and State equip it to withstand the storms of the tempest, which found expression on the European continent in the acute strife between the papacy and the rising kingdom of Italy, in Germany in the furious *Kulturkampf* of Bismarck against the Roman Catholic Church, and in France in the protracted and embittered controversy culminating in separation of Church and State in 1906?

At the end of the Napoleonic wars, indeed, there seemed more than a possibility of similar extreme measures of hostility between Church and State in England. The position of the established Church, with its accumulating abuses on the one hand and its obsolete claims to exclusive privilege on the other, invited not only the opposition of Protestant Dissenters and Roman Catholics, but the inveterate contumely of the Utilitarian school of thinkers. Nor was the danger confined to the Church of England; for some of the leading propagandists of this school had little respect for the Christian tradition in any of its corporate expressions. Accordingly, the several Churches began to construct defences against the possibility of an aggressive campaign and antipathetic temper on the part of the State. The Oxford Movement itself was primarily a protest and safeguard against this danger; not only was it occasioned by the action of the temporal power in reducing the number of Irish bishoprics according to its own determination and without consultation of the Church; but its *raison d'être* was to provide the clergy with a basis for their claims in case disestablishment should come upon them. In the first of the *Tracts for the Times*—written as R. W. Church averred 'like the short, rapid utterances of men in pain and danger and pressing emergency'—this note was clearly sounded. The importance of this protest received recognition from an unexpected quarter, when Professor Laski compared the Oxford Movement with the contemporaneous Scottish Disruption in precisely this respect. 'It is not a little curious that more attention should not have been paid to the remarkable analogy between the Oxford Movement and the Disruption of 1834 in the established Church of Scotland. Each was essentially an anti-Erastian movement. It was against an all-absorptive state that each group of men was contending. . . . In each case, as was well enough admitted by contemporaries, the attempt was made . . . to work out a doctrine of the Church which, neglecting the State, gave the Church the general organization of a perfect society.' There were of course important differences between the two movements; for that of Oxford was essentially clerical and challenged the State only indirectly; whereas that in Scotland was an assertion of the rights of the laity in the Church and a direct challenge to the State. But in principle, both movements were awakening their respective Churches to the need for a high doctrine of the sovereignty and autonomy of the Church, in virtue of its commission from Christ and His promise that the gates of hell should not prevail against it. The Crown rights of the Redeemer became the principle and war-cry of an awakened church-consciousness on all sides.

For the tension was not confined to established Churches. The re-establishment by Pius IX in 1850 of a territorial Roman Catholic hierarchy in England provoked an astonishing outburst of anti-papal fury in the country (fanned, it must be allowed, by the flamboyant language of Cardinal Wiseman). Indeed the attention of our forefathers in the year of the Great Exhibition seemed almost equally divided between the welcome of foreign visitors to the triumphs of that spectacle and the repulse of papal aggression! Lord John Russell induced the Whig administration of the time, despite the opposition of Gladstone, to pass an Ecclesiastical Titles Act, forbidding the proposed action of Rome. Notwithstanding, the Roman Catholic episcopate was reconstituted with territorial titles; the act was never enforced; and was itself quietly repealed by Gladstone's ministry in 1871. The victory of the kingdom of fairies over the temporal power was none the less real for being unobtrusive. It would have been well for Disraeli if he had read the signs of the times and learned the lesson of this episode. For being called upon, when his administration succeeded that of Gladstone, to deal with a popular outcry against the ceremonial eccentricities of the *epigoni* of the Tractarian revival, he had recourse to the passing of the Public Worship Regulation Act of 1874 to suppress these practices by coercive means. In this case, indeed, the act was enforced; and a number of clergymen suffered imprisonment for offending against its provisions. But the execution of the measure broke down, when it became plain that there was no means of releasing offenders from prison save at the risk of their re-incarceration for repetition of disobedience. Once again the kingdom of fairies had come off victorious in conflict with the state.

Much more serious were the results of the long controversy between Anglicans and Nonconformists concerning the provision by the state of primary education for all its citizens. For the passive resistance campaign to the Balfour Education Act of 1902, led by Dr. John Clifford, the famous Baptist pastor, threatened the spectacle of imprisonment or distraint of goods against Free Church ministers, and of a frontal collision between Church and State. Indeed this movement might have attained formidable proportions, but for the defeat of the Conservative government in the general election of 1906, and the return of a Liberal administration pledged to remedy the grievances of the resisters. It is easy to dismiss these melancholy education controversies as simply an unusually virulent manifestation of the traditional *odium theologicum*. But there was a vital principle at stake. For the supersession of the liberalism of the nineteenth century national state, with its adoption of the maxim of Cavour of *A Free Church in a Free State*, by the contemporary totalitarian tyrannies has set forth in large letters which he who runs may read, the peril of the control of all stages of public education by a power resolved to suppress freedom of thought and to inculcate a this-worldly ideology of its own devising. It was a sound instinct on the part of Nonconformists which seized upon education as a critical field for the relations of Church and State. Fortunately the English genius for compromise seems in this case to have attained a practical solution. For on the one hand, it is doubtful whether in the present century voluntaryism can hope to withstand the armoury of the modern *Leviathan*; and on the other hand recent experience has indicated that the State, like nature, abhors a vacuum; so that if it casts off alliance with the true religion, it will substitute some secular ideology of a purely temporal relevance. By the maintenance on the one side of an established Church both in England and Scotland together with complete religious liberty and civil equality for other Churches, and on the other side by the provisions of the Butler Education Act of 1944, and the sympathetic religious policy of the British Broadcasting Corporation, the English tradition may be held to have discovered at least a *modus vivendi* and at best a harmonious co-operation between twentieth century *Leviathan* and the kingdom of fairies.

23. THE SOCIAL GOSPEL

'I CANNOT understand what is the good of a national Church,' wrote Thomas Arnold in 1832, 'if it be not to Christianize the nation and introduce the principles of Christianity into men's social and civil relations; and expose the wickedness of that spirit which seems to think that there is no such sin as covetousness; and that if a man is not dishonest, he has nothing to do but make all the profit of his capital that he can.' Here was a new note, and one which was to become increasingly vocal and dominant in English religion in the nineteenth century. That century was indeed an era of revolution; but perhaps in no sphere was its revolutionary character more marked than in the changing attitude of the Churches towards social problems. Of course there had been outstanding examples of Christian philanthropy in earlier centuries, such as have been described in previous talks on the charity schools and hospitals of the eighteenth century, or the factory acts of the early nineteenth century. But during the latter half of the last century, there was a fundamental change in the approach of the Churches towards what became known as 'the-condition-of-the-people-question'. Generally speaking, the traditional attitude had been to regard the poor and indigent members of society as fulfilling their proper place in the divinely-ordered system of social classes, and providing the means for the exercise of the virtue of charity by individual wealthy Christians. The new approach was to regard the problem of the cure of poverty as corporate, not individual; a matter for the State not for private benefaction; and for the Churches to consider the application of the principles of Christian ethics to society and the State, and to demand social policies which were in accordance with the second great commandment, to love one's neighbour as oneself.

Perhaps the watershed between the old and new conceptions may be traced to the work of the Christian Socialists, led by Frederick Denison Maurice who gathered around him a small band of zealous enthusiasts. For Maurice, co-operation, not competition, was the divine law of the universe; and Socialism to be true to its ideals must be Christianized. 'Competition is put forth as the law of the universe,' he wrote; 'that is a lie; the time is come for us to declare that it is a lie by word and deed.' And again: 'The watchword of the Socialist is co-operation; the watchword of the anti-Socialist is competition. Anyone who recognizes the principle of co-operation as a stronger and truer principle than that of competition has a right to the honour or disgrace of being called a Socialist.' Maurice and his followers were prophets before their time; and if their practical attempts to translate their ideals into working systems, such as the Tailors' Working Association, failed because they were premature, the principles which they preached were to be fruitful and germinative. Within the established Church, the change in attitude was to become little short of revolutionary. Small groups such as the Guild of St. Matthew, the Church Socialist League, and the Christian Social Union, worked as leaven to influence official church opinion; and the remarkable extent of their success was strikingly shown in the Report of an Archbishops' Commission on 'Christianity and Industrial

Problems' in 1918, out of which sprang the Industrial Christian Fellowship.

Side by side with this steady, if slow, evolution of opinion within the established Church, went a stronger current of Christian influence on social problems through the Free Churches. It is one of the fortunate peculiarities of the English religious tradition that the political parties of the left, first the Liberal and then the Labour Party, have been to a very considerable degree influenced directly by Christian individuals and principles. The very divisions of Protestantism have helped this permeation. For example, when during the first half of the nineteenth century the Methodists suffered a series of severe secessions, these schisms, notably that of the Primitive Methodists and even more pronouncedly that of William Booth which led to the foundation of the Salvation Army, enabled Trades Unionism and Chartism to find leaders and counsellors amongst Christian ministers and laity. During the long leadership of the Liberal Party by Gladstone, there developed the phenomenon known as 'the Nonconformist conscience', by which the influence of the Free Churches became more closely and directly associated with the social reforms of that party. The employment by these Churches of lay preachers, moreover, furnished a generation of trades' union leaders with experience as speakers. In the persons of Liberal members of parliament, such as Thomas Burt, the miners' leader, and Joseph Arch, founder of the Agricultural Workers' Union, representatives of the working classes first gained entry to Westminster; and the first Labour member of the House of Commons, Keir Hardie, was a member of the Evangelical Union. Nor has the succession ceased in more recent times. Methodism contributed to the Labour administrations between the two wars of this half-century, Arthur Henderson, who occupied the positions of both Home and Foreign Secretary successively; whilst the present Labour Party has recently lost by the death of Mr. George Tomlinson, a minister of state of like religious persuasion. Anti-clerical parties have been unknown in English political life thus far, a circumstance due in no small measure to the peculiar genius and characteristics of the English religious tradition. During this same period, the action of Cardinal Manning in the London Dockers' Strike of 1889 brought the Roman Catholic Church into the foreground of social issues; and the series of encyclicals of Leo XIII and succeeding popes dealing with social problems, have found ready champions and exponents amongst leading English Roman Catholics.

The present half-century has witnessed, moreover, despite the manifold troubles of its course, a considerable strengthening of the interest in social problems within all the Churches, and a remarkable degree of co-operation in this field. After the end of the first world war, a noteworthy conference on politics, economics, and citizenship was held, after four years' preparatory study by various commissions, under the chairmanship of William Temple, later Archbishop successively of York and Canterbury. This conference, representative of all the English Churches except the Roman Catholic, made an extensive survey of the problems of contemporary society, and laid the foundations and principles for further study and action. Throughout this period also the Quakers have maintained their traditional pre-eminence in various manifold social services, especially during war-time and amongst the victims of economic distress and the uprooting of entire communities of refugees. In addition the British Jews have played a leading part in succouring their co-religionists who suffered an unprecedented persecution and expatriation in Europe. With the establishment in Great Britain since the end of the second world war of the Welfare State, Christian influence on social problems has perforce taken new forms. Not the least remarkable of contemporary phenomena has been the acceptance by all the Churches, established and non-established, of the principles of the Welfare State. To this end not a little must be ascribed to the influence of William Temple, who possessed the unusual combination of abilities to interpret Christianity in terms of social policy to his fellow-churchmen on the one hand, and to persuade political reformers on the other hand of the relevance of the Christian gospel to their social problems. Despite the irreparable loss suffered by all the Churches in his premature death, he being dead yet speaketh. For if the Victorian caricature of the Church of England as 'the Conservative Party at prayer' is almost ludicrously inapplicable to its present situation, and if the 'Nonconformist conscience' has ceased to be allied with one particular political party, it is because Christian influence has succeeded to so remarkable a degree in permeating the personnel and principles of both parties in the State. During the last century indeed the growth and influence of a Christian social conscience have gone far to fulfil Charles Kingsley's insistence that the Churches' primary task was to 'justify God to the people'.

24. SCIENCE, HISTORY, AND RELIGION

I falter where I firmly trod,
And falling with my weight of cares
Upon the world's great altar-stairs,
That slope thro' darkness up to God.

I stretch lame hands of faith, and grope,
And gather dust and chaff, and call,
To what I feel is Lord of all,
And faintly trust the larger hope.

It is just over a hundred years since the publication of Tennyson's *In Memoriam*, from which these stanzas are taken; and probably no poem expressed more poignantly and faithfully the Victorian confusion arising from the impact of science and history on the traditional faith of the English people. For during the latter half of the nineteenth century, Christian theology was subjected to a series of assaults which threatened the *bouleversement* of nearly all its traditional beliefs. The rumblings of the storm indeed had begun at least as early as 1830 by the publication of Charles Lyell's *Principles of Geology*, which burst violently the bounds of that chronology of the Bible, compiled by a seventeenth century Irish Archbishop, James Ussher, by showing that the history of the earth itself stretched far behind and beyond the four thousand years of this reckoning. Almost a generation later, Lyell followed up his earlier discoveries by his *Evidence of the Antiquity of Man*, published in 1863, which established the beginnings of the human race at a time and place far different from the account in Genesis.

These however were but the preliminaries of the tempest; the full force of which was felt with devastating effect on the appearance in 1859 of Charles Darwin's *Origin of Species.* It was this which laid the axe to the root of the tree of traditional Christian anthropology; for by applying the principles of evolution by natural selection to explain the development of animate creation and the emergence of *homo sapiens* from the lower animals, it challenged at once the Christian belief in a special creation of Adam and Eve together with the Genesis story of the Fall of Man in the garden of Eden. Man, instead of being created but a little lower than the angels, was alleged to have risen slowly and painfully from the lower animals; and with nature exhibiting fecundity of experiment combined with a ruthless lack of care for the casualties involved in the evolutionary process, even the status of man lost its former pre-eminence. Whereas the scientific movement of the seventeenth century had confirmed man in his proud position as the especial favourite of the Creator, its successor in the nineteenth century debased both his status in this world and his hope of the next. So, asked Tennyson, shall

> *Man, her last work, who seem'd so fair,*
> *Such splendid purpose in his eyes,*
> *Who roll'd the psalm to wintry skies*
> *And built him fanes of fruitless prayer.*
>
> *Who trusted God was Love indeed,*
> *And love Creation's final law—*
> *Though Nature red in tooth and claw*
> *With ravine, shriek'd against his creed—*
>
> *Who loved, who suffer'd countless ills,*
> *Who battled for the True, the Just,*
> *Be blown about the desert dust,*
> *Or seal'd within the iron hills?*

Thus Natural Science appeared to have challenged Christian belief to mortal combat from which one or other must emerge only by unconditional surrender. Moreover, worse was to come from another foe, when in 1865 E. B. Tylor published his *Researches into the Early History of Mankind,* which raised new issues relating to the origins of religion itself. From this study there developed the scientific investigation of the various natural religions of mankind, their striking similarities, and their humble origins in tribal taboos and animistic superstitions; and thus the entire field of research, known to the present century as the comparative study of religions, began to raise the doubt whether the Christian revelation with its prolegomena in Jewish religion, had anything unique in its origins or authoritative in its content. Back came the old deistic claims for natural religion against revelation; only this time natural religion was no longer the elevated and universal faith of man uncorrupted by priestcraft and churches, but a congeries of primitive customs and taboos, too crude and magical for educated men to think worthy of their consideration.

These, however, were attacks on revelation from without. Much more insidious were the assaults from within and the wounds received in the house of its friends. For the impact of historical criticism was even more far-reaching and important than that of scientific discovery since it challenged the claim of the Scriptural records themselves to accuracy. The dissolvent process which had been applied by secular historians to the legends of early Greece and Rome, was no less destructive when directed to the myths of Genesis. Furthermore, historical and literary critics were disputing the traditional authorship of the Pentateuch by Moses, suggesting that the Law contained in Deuteronomy and Leviticus had been evolved at a comparatively late date in Hebrew history, claiming for the eighth century prophets the honour of being the earliest books of the Old Testament, and relegating some of the Psalms to the post-exilic and even the Maccabean age. Such contentions were sufficiently startling in themselves; and even more disconcerting was the deduction that the religion of Israel had evolved slowly and with many setbacks from a primitive polytheism, or henotheism at best, to an ethical montheism, instead of having received this revelation at the outset. So early as 1830 Dean Milman in his *History of the Jews* had tried to prepare educated opinion in a purely general way for acceptance of Old Testament criticism, by explaining some of the miracles of its record as due to natural causation, by referring to Abraham as an oriental emir or sheik, and by remarking on the absence from his character of 'that nice and lofty sense of veracity which distinguishes a society where the point of honour has acquired a great influence'.

But if the results of Old Testament criticism were startling, those of the New Testament were alarming. When in 1846 George Eliot translated into English Strauss' *Leben Jesu*, educated opinion received a great shock from its negative conclusions. For Strauss virtually sacrificed not only the miracles, but also the historical credibility of the Gospels, regarding them as mythology cast in historical form. Similarly the appearance in 1863 of an English translation of Renan's *Vie de Jésus* deepened the prevailing apprehension. Two main lines of defence were essayed at first. On the one hand Dean Stanley and Benjamin Jowett tried to show that the religious value of the New Testament was unimpaired by critico-historical conclusions, since they could not diminish its appeal to the heart of the devout reader. On the other hand Sir John Seeley's *Ecce Homo* sought to point to the ethical teaching of Christ and his example as perfect Man, as being likewise untouched by critical questions. But the spade-work of serious and sustained rehabilitation of the authenticity and reliability of the New Testament books was carried out by a trio of Cambridge scholars, Lightfoot, Westcott, and Hort; whose painstaking, if unspectacular, studies steadied the faith of the educated, and restored a general feeling of confidence amongst Christians.

Of course there were casualties in the combat. A Congregationalist scholar, Dr. Samuel Davidson (now commemorated by a Theological Chair in the University of London), was dismissed from the Lancashire Independent College for his adoption of critical views of the Old Testament. An even greater *cause célèbre* was the dismissal of Professor Robertson Smith from his Chair at Aberdeen for similar opinions. In the Church of England, two of the contributors to a volume of *Essays and Reviews* were prosecuted for heresy, and saved only by the verdict of a civil supreme court of appeal, the Judicial Committee of the Privy Council. Gradually, however, alarm subsided and when a further composite book, *Lux Mundi*, appeared in 1889 from successors of the Tractarian tradition, it escaped censure, and even won general acceptance. Thus steadily, if slowly, the Churches adjusted themselves to the new scientific and historical discoveries of the nineteenth century. The achievement was remarkable; for Christian scholars had been called upon to essay, and to a considerable degree had succeeded in effecting, a re-examination and re-statement of their traditional beliefs, which was unprecedented and unparalleled in scope and character. If many faltered where before they firmly trod, there was gain as well as loss in the acceptance of a view of the Bible as the record of a progressive relevation in which God, who had spoken in times past and by divers manners to the fathers, had consummated this in the person of the historic Jesus, the Messiah, His Son.

25. MISSIONARY EXPANSION

WHEN John Wesley proclaimed the world to be his parish and when his intrepid colleague, George Whitefield, translated precept into practice by tireless journeys in the new world as well as the old, they were, albeit unwittingly, laying the foundations of the modern missionary movement which during the nineteenth and twentieth centuries has transformed the world by carrying the gospel to its remotest parts, and created a world-wide Christian Church. Indeed, perhaps the most remarkable outcome of the Evangelical revival of the eighteenth century was its impetus to the missionary vocation of the Church. Hitherto the burden of missionary work had been borne chiefly by the Roman Catholic Church, thanks to the colonial expansion of Spain, Portugal, and France, and to the new religious life and zeal generated by the Counter-Reformation. By contrast the several Churches in England had been comparatively unresponsive to the obligation to preach the gospel to all nations. Indeed the chief evangelistic work amongst natives sponsored by the Church of England during the eighteenth century had been undertaken in India under the auspices of the Society for Promoting Christian Knowledge (founded in 1698), but with missionaries drawn from the Lutheran Churches of Denmark and Germany. The Anglican Society for the Propagation of the Gospel (founded in 1701) had concerned itself mainly with English emigrants to the North American colonies and to India, and had confined its activities otherwise to the slaves working on its own plantations.

Amongst the Protestant Churches generally, the Moravians, or the *Unitas Fratrum* (in company with some of whose members John Wesley had crossed the Atlantic), were uniquely distinguished by the magnitude of their missionary enterprise.

With the penetration of the Evangelical revival, however, there came the beginnings of change. The honour of taking the lead in this field fell to the Baptists, in the person of William Carey, a shoemaker in the Midlands, who after becoming a Baptist pastor continued to eke out his scanty stipend by keeping a school. He first took seriously to heart the dominical command to make disciples of all nations and applied it to his own Church and condition. In 1792 therefore the Baptist Missionary Society was founded (the very year, be it noted in passing, in which Great Britain entered the long war against France); and in the following year Carey himself sailed for India, where he fulfilled an apostolate of more than forty years, labouring more abundantly than almost any other individual as evangelist, translator, educator, and social reformer. In 1795 the London Missionary Society was founded, whose peculiar and continuing characteristic was its undenominational charter; which declared its objective to be 'not to send Presbyterianism, Independency, Episcopacy, or any other form of Church Order or Government . . . but the glorious Gospel of the Blessed God to the Heathen; and that it shall be left to the minds of the persons whom God may call into the fellowship of His Son from among them, to assume for themselves such form of Church Government as to them shall appear most agreeable to the Word of God'. In accordance with these principles the Society was supported by Independents, Presbyterians, and some of the leading Anglican Evangelicals. In 1799, however, the last-named, under the leadership of Charles Simeon, established their own society, the Church Missionary Society. During the early decades of the nineteenth century also the Methodist Missionary Society was finally organized; and from the United States of America there came Baptist missions in Burma, and Congregationalist in India; whilst in 1824 the Foreign Missions Committee of the Church of Scotland began work in the Indian continent.

The movement which thus spread as it were by spontaneous combustion amongst the several Churches, expanded to such proportions as to make the nineteenth and first half of the twentieth centuries the greatest epoch of missionary enterprise in the history of the Christian Church. Moreover, the movement was characterized by new features. In contrast to earlier centuries, its work was inspired and financed by voluntary contributions and personal service of the Churches themselves rather than by the civil governments with which they were associated in Europe and America. Particularly noteworthy is the circumstance that the principal agency of these advances has been the missionary societies set up within the several Churches. Furthermore the last century and a half have been *par excellence* the era of Protestant expansion. Not indeed that the Roman Church has been indifferent or negligent; rather the Protestant Churches, having awoken to a realization of their responsibilities, have made rapid strides towards making up the leeway of past centuries. It is perhaps of especial interest to observe that the most prominent figure in the inception of the Roman Catholic Society for the Propagation of the Faith in the nineteenth century was a laywoman, Pauline Jaricot. Equally remarkable is the fact that this outburst of missionary activity has been achieved during a period in which many of the European countries, which have been the traditional strongholds of Christianity, have lapsed into scepticism or indifference on the one hand, or have been submerged by totalitarian anti-Christian tyrannies on the other hand.

The results of this missionary movement have been correspondent with the efforts devoted to its prosecution. In the Indian continent, in central Africa, in China and Japan, in the various islands of the seven seas, in the countries of the British Commonwealth, and throughout the continents of North and South America, Christianity has been propagated, planted, and taken root amidst a hitherto unprecedented number and variety of races and cultures. Never before had the gospel spread to so many and various peoples. Moreover, the objective has been, not the reproduction of Occidental traditions and customs, but the development of native, indigenous Churches, fostered inevitably during their early stages by contributions and personnel from Europe and America, but destined ultimately to become self-supporting and self-governing, and to be staffed by native ministers and teachers. Both Roman Catholic and Protestant founder-Churches have pursued this aim; and the evolution of native traditions of worship within the common heritage of faith and order has been attained in part, though much remains to be done. Evidently, a great part of the work has been only indirectly proselytizing in character; for hospitals, schools, and colleges have been founded by several Churches, primarily to raise the standards of health and literacy, and secondarily through these means to spread Christian beliefs and ideals by civilizing and cultural agencies rather than by direct evangelization. Accordingly one result of Christian missions has been the reducing to writing of more native languages than had attained literary form in all the previous history of mankind. The need for translations of the Bible and for the dissemination of Christian literature led to many tongues which had been hitherto illiterate, finding expression in written characters. Similarly, medical missions greatly reduced the toll of disease and illness, and helped to raise the physical standards of life amongst native races. An outstanding feature of the modern missionary expansion also has been the mass conversion to Christianity of primitive peoples, whether negroes of North America, or natives of Africa, of the Philippines, and of the East Indies (to mention but some of many examples); and most of these conversions have been from animistic forms of religion.

The magnitude of this achievement is aptly illustrated by the circumstance that Professor Latourette's *History of the Expansion of Christianity* from the apostolic age to the present century, allots three volumes to the hundred years between 1815 and 1914 out of a total of seven volumes. 'In geographic extent,' runs his verdict, 'in movements issuing from it, and in its effect upon the race, in the nineteenth century Christianity had a far larger place in human history than at any previous time.' Or again: 'Never had the faith won adherents among so many peoples and in so many countries. Never had it exerted so wide an influence upon the human race. Measured by geographic extent and the effect upon mankind as a whole, the nineteenth century was the greatest thus far in the history of Christianity.' Not even the tragic effects of two world wars have arrested its progress; though the present half-century has witnessed severe setbacks. It is with equal surprise perhaps and comfort that the student of history realizes that the most recent century of Christian history has been the most outstanding in its conquests. The faith which led William Carey and other pioneers to expect great things of God has been abundantly justified by experience and results.

26. THE ANGLICAN COMMUNION

THE great missionary expansion of the nineteenth century was a response of all the Churches to the challenge of a new situation; and its effects were marked on their internal development and external relations. Of no Church is this more true than of the Church of England. For the nineteenth century witnessed the expansion of what had been by comparison an ecclesiastical city of Zoar into the worl-wide Anglican Communion. Nor was its geographical extension the most remarkable feature of this change. By its means Anglicanism was transformed from a national faith into a universal interpretation of Christianity, seeking to commend its standards of belief, worship, and practice to natives of Africa, India, various islands scattered amongst the oceans, and far Eastern countries. Though its membership is considerably exceeded by other Churches, it has established its claim to present a version of Christianity which has its distinctive contribution to make to the Church Universal of the future.

As has been observed already, it was the Evangelical revival of the latter half of the eighteenth century which rekindled the zeal of the Church of England for missionary activity. Hitherto its only missionary society, the S.P.G., had concerned itself principally with the spiritual welfare of English colonists in North America and India. With the rebellion of the American colonies and their constitution as the United States of America, they passed outside the sphere of the S.P.G. Instead they created the Protestant Episcopal Church in the United States, forming thus the earliest branch of what had not yet become the Anglican Communion. Moreover, as a result of the emigration of a number of loyalists to Canada, the first Anglican overseas bishopric was established in Nova Scotia in 1787, from which has developed the Church of England in Canada. At the present time the Protestant Episcopal Church in the United States has a hundred and twelve bishoprics, including its missionary dioceses; whilst its sister Church in Canada and Newfoundland has twenty-seven bishoprics, grouped into four provinces, each under its own archbishop.

Meantime a second British Empire was in process of foundation in India, Australasia, and South Africa; and thither too the Church of England likewise spread. It was due to the untiring efforts of William Wilberforce that the East India Company's Charter was altered in 1813 in order to authorize missionary work and the establishment of a bishopric at Calcutta. From this modest beginning there have developed the sixteen bishoprics of the Church of India, Burma, and Ceylon, four of which, however, left the parent-Church in 1947 to become members of the newly-created Church of South India. In 1813 Australia was designated as an archdeaconry under the jurisdiction of the see of Calcutta! To-day the Anglican Church there is represented by twenty-one dioceses organized in four provinces; whilst in the neighbouring islands of New Zealand, there is a single province with nine dioceses, including those of Polynesia and Melanesia. In like manner the Church of the Province of South Africa embraces fourteen dioceses under the archbishopric of Capetown; and in various parts of tropical Africa bishoprics have been planted, the most recent development of which has been the constitution in 1951 of the Province of West Africa, embracing five dioceses. In other parts of the world as in China, Japan and the adjacent islands, bishoprics have been founded under the direct jurisdiction of the see of Canterbury. During the last one hundred and seventy years, therefore, more than two hundred and fifty dioceses of the Anglican Communion have been established; and the Church of England has thereby become the parent of a considerable and various progeny.

Furthermore, the Anglican Communion has developed certain characteristic features which are both of intrinsic interest and of considerable importance for the ecumenical movement of the present and future. First, the several provinces have all accepted the ideal of a constitutional episcopacy, governing with the counsel and consent of representative bodies of their clergy and laity; and the great majority have embodied this ideal in working constitutions, with the diocesan synod at the base and provincial synods or councils at the apex. By a happy combination of precedents from the early history of the Church with improvisations suited to local needs and circumstances, the Anglican Communion has thus made an original and valuable contribution to constitutional evolution. Secondly, its several provinces meet every ten years in a Conference of bishops at Lambeth Palace, the London home of the Archbishops of Canterbury, for consultation and deliberation. Beginning in 1867 these Lambeth Conferences have attained an unique position of influence in the Anglican Communion. Their authority indeed is recommendatory, not mandatory; and their resolutions are not binding on the various provinces and dioceses represented. There is thus nothing approaching either a coercive power of the Lambeth Conference, nor a quasi-Anglican papacy in the new position of the see of Canterbury. But the conclusions of these episcopal conferences nevertheless possess a considerable importance, arising from their intrinsic value and from the Cyprianic conception of the episcopate which they imply. Thirdly, the Anglican Communion, like the British Commonwealth of Nations, is held together rather by a general acceptance of and loyalty to a common tradition of belief, worship, and practice than by a closely defined system of doctrine, liturgy, and discipline. The threefold cord which binds together the Church of England, namely the Book of Common Prayer, the Ordinal, and the Articles of Religion, likewise constitutes a band of cohesion within the Anglican Communion. But within this framework, there is wide latitude and variety of local custom and usage. The Church of England in its relations with the other parts of the Anglican Communion has followed the sapient advice of Pope Gregory the Great to Augustine of Canterbury, concerning the adoption and adaptation of local custom and habit and the avoidance of a rigid uniformity. Thus the Church of the Province of South Africa has revised its Communion Office and is proceeding with the revision of other parts of its Prayer Book. Similarly, the inclusion of the Thirty-Nine Articles is no longer insisted upon in all parts of the Anglican Communion; for it is held with justice that some of the controversies to which they relate are foreign to the conditions of native Churches outside European countries. Thus local experiment and variation are encouraged, subject to a general allegiance to the fundamental position of the Church of England.

It is worthy of passing notice that the outspreading of the Anglican Communion, like the wider nineteenth century missionary expansion of which it is a part, owes much to the work of missionary societies. Foremost amongst these are the Society for the Propagation of the Gospel, and the Church Missionary Society; whilst other smaller sodalities have promoted missionary work in specific and particular areas, such, for example, as the Cambridge Mission to Delhi and the Universities Mission to Central Africa. By this means also the comprehensive nature of the Anglican tradition, embracing the three schools of churchmanship, Anglo-Catholic, Evangelical, and Liberal, has been reproduced in various parts of the Anglican Communion, though this has occasioned problems and difficulties by no means easy of solution. Thus the Anglican Communion has played its part in the fulfilment of the missionary vocation of the Christian Church, which has been so characteristic a feature of the history of the last century and a half. Thereby it has established also its claim to possess and to present a version of Christianity, which has its own valuable and distinctive contribution to make to the ecumenical movement of the present and the future.

27. MODERNISM AND LIBERAL PROTESTANTISM

As the nineteenth century gave place to the twentieth, the unsettlement caused by the movement of historical criticism of the Bible (of which I spoke in an earlier talk) seemed to have subsided, and the victory to rest with the critics. But the calm was the prelude to a greater storm; for the application of critical principles to the traditional Christology of the Church was yet to be undertaken, and it was a task not to be essayed without grave peril and conflict. The general atmosphere, however, seemed congenial to the venture; and with the accession of Leo XIII to the papal chair, and his elevation of John Henry Newman to the cardinalate, the breezes of what was later to be known as 'Modernism' seemed to have dispelled the mists traditionally surrounding the rock of Peter. For

Newman had demonstrated that the classical theology of the Church was the result of a long process of development. Critical attention was now to be given to the earliest stages of that development, namely within the New Testament itself.

Generally speaking, the centre of interest shifted to what became known as 'the quest of the historical Jesus'; that is, to the attempt to discover, behind the framework of Christian theology and even behind the interpretations in the Gospels and Epistles themselves, the teaching, person, and facts of the life of Jesus of Nazareth. By paring off the refractory elements of later theological explanations and ecclesiastical tradition, it was hoped to come face to face with the Jesus of history. This quest gave birth to two divergent, even contradictory, movements, those of Liberal Protestantism and of Roman Catholic Modernism. The leaders of each camp were at first foreign scholars; Adolf von Harnack among Liberal Protestants and the Abbé Alfred Loisy amongst the Modernists. The publication in 1901 of Harnack's *Das Wesen des Christentums* (translated into English as *What is Christianity?*) began the contest. In this book, Harnack set forth three main positions; first, that in Jesus' teaching the Kingdom of God was an individual, interior and spiritual allegiance; secondly, that the essence of the gospel lay in the Fatherhood of God and the realization offered to each individual of his sonship to God, again a conception individual and not ecclesiastical in character; and thirdly that the core of Christology lay in the unique consciousness by Jesus of his own especial and peculiar sonship to God, which was the basis of his claim to Messiahship. From these principal points, Harnack concluded that Christianity was originally and essentially an individual, spiritual and mystical religion; from which the traditional Catholic system of Church, priesthood, and sacraments was a declension and perversion. His summary was stated in moving words: 'The Christian religion is something simple and sublime; it means one thing and one thing only; eternal life in the midst of time, by the strength and under the eyes of God.'

In reply to this, Loisy, by *L'Évangile et L'Église*, sought to establish an entire contradiction. He insisted that Christ himself was known only by tradition, and that this tradition, as shown in primitive Christianity, disproved Harnack's position. For Loisy, Jesus' teaching about the Kingdom of God was objective, collective, and future, to be realized when He came again within the lifetime of his first disciples to inaugurate the supernatural and eschatological kingdom. So also Loisy insisted that for Jesus, Messiahship meant the rule in a visible, objective, and apocalyptic kingdom. But instead of this expected speedy return in glory, there had come the resurrection of Jesus and the foundation of the Church. 'Jesus foretold the kingdom,' he wrote, 'and it was the Church that came.' So the dogma, the sacraments, and the hierarchy of the Church were developments, under the guidance indeed of the Holy Spirit, from this historical situation; but present only implicitly, and not expressly, in the teaching of Jesus. In later explanations of his book, Loisy made explicit its purport by emphasizing, for example, that the historical Jesus was not omniscient, and that his resurrection was not properly speaking a fact of the historical order, but of the spiritual and supra-historical order. Undoubtedly Loisy had answered Harnack; but he had done so by declaring dark sentences and advancing novel and revolutionary hypotheses.

Both these schools of thought had representatives in England. Modernism was upheld particularly by Father George Tyrrell, a Jesuit, and by the lay nobleman Baron von Hügel. Tyrrell, like Loisy, tried to reconcile traditional Christian theology and modern criticism by accepting the eschatological view of the teaching of Jesus, which had been widely canvassed by Albert Schweitzer in *The Quest of the Historical Jesus*. Tyrrell argued in *Christianity at the Cross-Roads*, that 'the Christ of eschatology is substantially the same as the Christ of catholic tradition and experience, that is, a supernatural, otherworldly, transcendent, essentially mysterious Christ'. Both Loisy and Tyrrell, together with other leading Modernist priests, suffered excommunication; a fate which Baron von Hügel escaped chiefly because he was a layman, and also because the Roman Catholic authorities in England were aware of the sensation which such a step would have created in educated circles. When therefore the storm broke, von Hügel sought to rally his followers around his own threefold fortress of critical opinions in Biblical study, cultivation of the mystical element in religion, and loyalty to the institutional Church, its sacraments and discipline.

Within the Church of England and the Free Churches,

Liberal Protestantism was the prevalent fashion during the first two decades of the present century. A group of Oxford scholars strove to reconstruct the *Foundations* of faith whilst surrendering many outposts. The historicity of the miracles of the New Testament was much disputed; and the question of the legitimate degree of latitude allowed in subscription to the creeds was the subject of vehement discussion. Amongst the Free Churches, Dr. R. J. Campbell, minister of the City Temple, set forth *The New Theology* in forceful and persuasive terms, and maintained for some years the position of principal protagonist for Liberal Protestantism. When he received ordination in the Church of England, his mantle fell upon Dr. W. E. Orchard, who beginning from an advanced Liberalism in theology, developed into an equally strong orthodoxy of belief until he came finally to rest in the Church of Rome.

Both Modernism and Liberal Protestantism had raised fundamental issues of Biblical scholarship and theology, concerning the character of twentieth century restatement and reinterpretation of traditional Christian doctrine. Within the Roman Catholic Church indeed the critical movement was suppressed by the anti-Modernist Oath imposed by Pius X, by the condemnation of individual Modernists and of Modernism generally in the encyclical *Pascendi*, and by the series of pronouncements of the Biblical Commission established at Rome on the authorship and date of the several books of the Old and New Testaments, which in general contradicted the conclusions of scholars. Within the Church of England and the Free Churches, the debate has continued; and a remarkable reaction has set in during the inter-war period and since, against the standpoint no less than the detailed conclusions of earlier scholars. New influences from the continent, particularly that of Karl Barth, have turned the tide of Liberal Protestantism, and rehabilitated a new Biblical theology. Generally speaking, it may be said that the doctrine of the Church has been considerably revived and re-emphasized; that the eschatological element in the New Testament has been rationalized in the concept of 'realized eschatology'; and that recognition has been accorded to the fact that the Kingdom of God in history is both present and future, partly realized here and now, and wholly to be fulfilled in the hereafter. A new 'theology of crisis' has supplanted the quest of the historical Jesus; and the Churches have essayed the task of restoring orthodoxy in a world less antipathetic to the claims of mystery and authority than the generation which flourished before 1914.

28. THE ECUMENICAL MOVEMENT AND THE PROBLEMS OF REUNION

DURING the greater part of the period covered by these talks, the several Churches in England have been more conscious perhaps of their differences, even of their conflicts, than of their unity. The twentieth century has seen a remarkable reversal of this situation; and probably the most outstanding characteristic of its ecclesiastical history thus far has been the growth and momentum of the movement towards reunion. Not indeed that this tendency has been peculiar or confined to the British Isles. Rather, as my title indicates, it is an ecumenical or world-wide movement and it has sprung chiefly from the missionary activity of the last century. For when the several Churches of Europe expanded into world-wide communions, they found that many of the divisions deeply stamped on their own history and development, were almost unintelligible to non-European converts, unfamiliar with the controversies of the Reformation and subsequent centuries. If Christianity was to come to these converts as a unifying and integrating influence, the chronic divisions of Christendom must be healed; and as great a degree of co-operation and unity as possible be achieved. Furthermore, the emergence within Europe itself and the transplantation to the East, of powerful anti-Christian states, particularly the totalitarian tyrannies of Marxism and Nazi-ism, has confronted the Churches of the old world with a challenge, to which only their united forces, both at home and abroad, might hope to be equal. Accordingly the ecumenical movement, which has arisen as a response to this challenge, has made rapid and remarkable progress in this present half-century.

At home, small beginnings had been made amongst the several Churches themselves, by the decennial Lambeth Conferences, the formation of the Presbyterian Alliance, the decennial

Methodist Ecumenical Conferences, and similar movements on the part of the Congregationalists and Baptists; and by the setting-up of the National Council of the Free Churches. After the first world war also there came the striking phenomena of the union of the Presbyterian Churches in Scotland and the reunion of the Methodists. Yet all these were but the first trickles of what has developed into a mighty stream.

Perhaps the first considerable stirring of the waters may be seen in the Edinburgh Conference of 1910, to which indeed long and arduous preparatory work had been prefaced, and which owed much to the influence of such societies as the Student Christian Movement and the World's Student Christian Federation. Many pregnant issues of ecumenical character were debated at this gathering; but probably the most significant appeal emerging from its deliberations was that for unity amongst the several Churches represented. The first world war interrupted its work and preparations for further conferences; but during the interval between 1919 and 1939 two such further gatherings were held, at Jerusalem in 1928 and at Tambaram near Madras in 1938. The choice of these places of assembly and the composition of the delegations, emphasized the increasing influence and importance of the Churches in Asia and Africa. Necessarily, these conferences were occupied with many other matters of urgency besides that of reunion. Therefore other and ancillary movements concerned themselves more specifically with detailed problems of reunion; particularly the conferences on Life and Work, and on Faith and Order, sponsored by leading churchmen from Europe, America and Great Britain, and meeting for discussion of theological and ecclesiastical differences between their several Churches.

A notable step forward was taken at the Lambeth Conference of 1920, by the issue of its *Appeal to all Christian People,* which not only made a moving plea for organic unity but put forward practical suggestions for its realization. These included the so-called Lambeth Quadrilateral, a four-point programme, embracing acceptance of the Scriptures as the rule and ultimate standard of faith; of the Nicene creed as the sufficient statement of the Christian faith; of the sacraments of Baptism and Holy Communion; and of a ministry acknowledged by every part of the Church as possessing not only the inward call of the Spirit but also the commission of Christ and the authority of the whole body: which the authors of the Appeal identified with the historic episcopate. This initiative led to a series of conversations with other Churches, both at home and abroad. Some practical results were obtained, though of a severely limited nature. For example, some of the autocephalous Churches of the Eastern Orthodox Church recognized the validity of Anglican Orders and thereby opened the way for a degree of intercommunion. Anglican bishops have participated in the consecration of bishops of the Church of Sweden, and *vice versa*; and here also a limited measure of intercommunion has been established between the two Churches. Full intercommunion has been attained between the Church of England and the Old Catholic Churches of the continent. But conversations with the Free Churches at home, though cordial in tone and registering welcome advances in mutual understanding and sympathy, have not progressed yet to the point of intercommunion. Accordingly, after the second world war the present Archbishop of Canterbury, seeking to discover whether a basis for intercommunion might be established through the adoption by the Free Churches of episcopacy within their own communions, inaugurated a further series of conversations. The result of these conferences, set forth in a recent *Report on Church Relations in England*, is at present under consideration by the participating Churches.

Meantime continuous study has been promoted of the principal differences of confessional standards, church order, liturgy, and discipline, which separate the Churches; and their results have been considered in a series of conferences, such as those of Life and Work at Stockholm and Fänø, and of Faith and Order at Lausanne and Lund, which have co-ordinated and carried forward the task. But undoubtedly the most spectacular and successful recent advance has been the inauguration of the World Council of Churches, with a subsection in this country known as the British Council of Churches. Within the operations of the World Council and its various departments, there has been set up a practical organization for mutual conference, counsel, and co-operation in a wide variety of spheres. But the World Council of Churches, though aspiring to the ideal of an ultimate reunion, does not conceive of itself as an immediate agent for effecting this objective. It accepts its constituent members as churches, but realizing the number and importance of the issues dividing them, does not seek any short-cut to organic union.

Notwithstanding, the progress during the present half-century in the sphere of unity between the Churches has been considerable, and in view of their past history, phenomenal. Undoubtedly the most important and audacious advance has been the creation in 1947 of the Church of South India; in which non-episcopal and episcopal Churches have united on the basis of acceptance of the fact of the historic episcopate without any particular theological interpretation being required. During the quinquennium of its history, this Church has made rapid steps towards internal unity and consolidation; and may well prove a pointer and portent towards further schemes of ecclesiastical union. Moreover, at home signs multiply of the readiness of some non-episcopal Churches to accept episcopacy as a condition of organic union, provided that this does not involve any breach in their intercommunion with other non-episcopal Churches, and that satisfactory provision can be made for the co-existence side by side during an interim period of presbyterally- and episcopally-ordained ministries. Whilst there are many unsolved problems and unsurmounted obstacles in the road to reunion, it would seem that a great door and effectual has been opened by the ecumenical movement of the twentieth century.

29. ANGLICAN-ROMAN APPROACHES

FROM the ecumenical movement, which was the subject of my last talk, the Church of Rome has stood aloof. Its exclusive claims have not allowed it to send official delegates to any inter-confessional conferences, though upon occasion it has been represented by observers. Nor did the two and a half centuries of internecine strife from 1570 to 1829 between the Church of England and Rome afford fruitful soil for the cultivation of friendly rapprochement. Nevertheless, even before the Oxford Movement rekindled interest in and attraction for the

Roman Catholic Church in Anglican circles, sporadic attempts had been made towards an amicable discussion of points of difference. During the reign of Charles I, a convert from Anglicanism, Christopher Davenport (known in religion as Franciscus a Sancta Clara) examined the Thirty-Nine Articles from the standpoint of the decrees of the Council of Trent. His conclusions were that nineteen of these Articles *in extenso* together with parts of five others were wholly in agreement with Roman doctrine; that nine others and parts of two further Articles were patient of a favourable interpretation; whilst six Articles and parts of three others were beyond his capacity to reconcile with the Tridentine definitions. His essay was interesting as a pioneer attempt to consider divergencies dispassionately and irenically.

The next serious endeavour towards mutual understanding was undertaken by more responsible and weighty theologians, in a correspondence between Archbishop Wake of Canterbury and two doctors of the Sorbonne, Dr. Du Pin and Dr. Girardin in the early eighteenth century. Although this interchange of learned treatises produced no practical results, it inspired on the Anglican side a defence of English episcopal consecrations and ordinations combined with a firm assertion of the grounds for repudiating papal supremacy, and from the Roman side a further Commentary from Du Pin on the Thirty-Nine Articles in relation to the decrees of Trent. It is important to observe that the first anticipations of the position later to be adopted by Newman in *Tract XC* had come from the Roman side in the persons of Davenport and Du Pin.

It was, however, the Oxford Movement which brought a new interest in and appreciation of the problem of Anglo-Roman relations. In 1865 Dr. Pusey published an *Eirenicon* in order to state, and if possible to bridge, the differences between the two Churches. The Vatican Council of 1870, however, by its definition of the papal *magisterium* and its promulgation of papal infallibility raised new obstacles and retarded Dr. Pusey's hopes. It was not until a chance meeting occurred in 1889 between Viscount Halifax, a leading Anglo-Catholic layman, and a French scholar, the Abbé Portal, that a new venture was tried. This took the form of a suggestion that a joint-commission of Roman and Anglican scholars should examine in a spirit of historical impartiality the limited question of Anglican

Orders, as a means towards the further discussion of the reunion of the respective Churches. Instead, however, Leo XIII in 1896 appointed an exclusively Roman commission to enquire into the matter. Its issue was the Bull *Apostolicae Curae,* declaring Anglican Orders invalid. This verdict rested on the historical facts that during the reign of Mary Tudor and in some subsequent cases, individuals ordained according to the Anglican Ordinal had been reordained by Rome; and on the theoretical ground that the Anglican Ordinal was defective in form and intention. In the former respect it was contended that there is no explicit form making clear the conferment of sacerdotal power to offer sacrifice for the living and the dead; and in the latter respect, that the Church of England did not intend to ordain a true priesthood nor to bestow the *summum sacerdotium* on its bishops. In reply the two English archbishops published an official *Responsio* in which they affirmed that their Church did 'truly teach the doctrine of the Eucharistic sacrifice', explained the nature of this teaching, and justified the forms for the Ordering of Priests and the Consecration of Bishops in the English Ordinal. Once again, the action of Rome had put an end to further discussion by constituting itself judge in a case to which it was also a party.

With the issue of the Lambeth Conference *Appeal to all Christian People* in 1920, Halifax and Portal determined to try to reopen discussions, by approaching Cardinal Mercier of Malines with the request that he would sponsor conferences between Anglicans and Roman Catholics on the general question of reunion. Accordingly in December, 1921, the first Conversation was held, attended on the Anglican side by Halifax, Dr. Armitage Robinson, Dean of Wells, and Dr. W. H. Frere, afterwards Bishop of Truro; and on the Roman side by the Cardinal, his Vicar-General Mgr. van Roey, and Portal. Its success encouraged the hope of further meetings, for which official recognition from Rome and Canterbury might be sought. On 22 November, 1922, Pius XI authorized Cardinal Gasparri to inform Mercier that 'the Holy See approves and encourages such conversations, and prays God with all its heart to bless them'. A corresponding recognition was given by the two English archbishops. At the second meeting in March, 1923, the participants discussed practical measures for regulating the position of the Anglican Communion within that of

Rome, if and when agreement had been reached on theological questions. Naturally, this seemed to many to be putting the cart before the horse; and when the Conversations were resumed in November, 1923, their personnel was increased by the addition on the Anglican side of Bishop Charles Gore and Dr. Kidd, Warden of Keble College, Oxford; and on the Roman side of Mgr. Pierre Batiffol and Canon Hemmer. At the insistence of the Archbishop of Canterbury they discussed the position of St. Peter in relation to the other apostles and of the pope in relation to the episcopate. At a fourth meeting in May, 1925, Mercier read an anonymous paper entitled 'The Church of England United but not Absorbed', which again turned discussion to the constitutional problems of uniting the two Communions. But the deaths of Mercier in January, 1926, and of Portal the following June, presaged the end of the Conversations. Moreover, the climate at Rome was becoming unfavourable; and the venture shortly petered out.

Notwithstanding, much surprise was occasioned in well-informed Anglican circles by the recent publication of some of the notes and correspondence of Mgr. Batiffol in which he had assured the papal nuncio in Paris in June, 1926, and the Pope himself in April, 1927, that the Conversations had never envisaged the corporate reunion of the Anglican and Roman Churches, but only the rapprochement of the Anglo-Catholics towards the Church of Rome. But the tenor of the Conversations made plain that the question of the union of the two Churches had been the subject of detailed discussion at two meetings, in one of which Mercier had produced the anonymous paper before mentioned on 'L'Église Anglicane Unie non Absorbée'. This tergiversation on the part of Batiffol therefore caused much astonishment and criticism, as did its evident motive in the changing climate of opinion at the Vatican. With the issue in January, 1928, by Pius XI of the Bull *Mortalium Animos* the Malines Conversation came to an end, and similar ventures were discouraged. Nor has the subsequent definition by Pius XII of the Assumption of the Virgin Mary as an article of faith contributed anything to a better understanding between members of the Church of Rome and of other Churches or to the hopes of mutual accommodation.

30. CHRISTIANITY IN THE CONTEMPORARY WORLD

THIS talk, which brings to an end the series on the English Religious Tradition, finds itself thereby cast for the melancholy rôle described by Alexander Pope:

A needless Alexandrine ends the song,
And, like a wounded snake, drags its slow length along.

The purpose of the series has been to sketch certain salient features of this tradition, and to indicate their influence on the development of Church, State, and Society during the last four centuries. It is pertinent therefore to ask what lessons the survey affords for a generation upon whom the end of the age has come? To essay an answer, indeed, involves forsaking the safer path of historical interpretation of the past for the perilous venture of prophecy concerning the future.

The English religious tradition has achieved a balance between recognition of the Christian character and profession of the State by the maintenance of an established Church in England and Scotland on the one hand, and full acknowledgement of the principle of liberty of conscience and freedom of religion for all its citizens on the other hand. This achievement in turn has delivered the nation from the growth of clerical and anticlerical parties in politics and from the penetration of its political life by anti-Christian ideologies. This in itself represents no mean achievement even though the result has been attained by a pragmatic process of trial and error rather than by the enunciation of abstract theories of the nature of political society. The English genius for compromise and for seeking practical solutions in preference to theoretical maxims has been justified by its fruits. But the question presses with urgent insistence whether this careful equipoise of variant tendencies can be maintained in an age, characterized in national affairs by the planned economy of the Welfare State, and in the international field by the challenge of aggressive secularist totalitarian despotisms. Do not these contemporary conditions presage the end of the give-and-take custom of English life;

and can the English religious tradition hope to withstand the pressure of the benevolent Welfare State at home and of the hostile totalitarian tyrannies abroad?

In the domestic sphere, it is undoubted that the basic principles of the Welfare State have been cordially welcomed and accepted by all the Churches, notwithstanding the fact that the process has involved the monopolizing by the State of a large field of social services hitherto chiefly operated by their voluntary enterprise. The Churches indeed have recognized that the Welfare State has gone far towards realizing the aspirations of the Christian Socialists of the nineteenth century. Moreover, each of the principal political parties to-day, Conservative, Labour, and Liberal, contains active groups of practising Christians whose concerted aim is to act as leaven influencing the policies of their respective parties. But the Welfare State, like its predecessors, whether tribal, feudal, monarchical, or democratic, can only carry its policies into effect through the agency of individuals, to whom is entrusted the administrative and executive function of translating principles into practice. If in the past the ' charity ' of the Churches too easily and too often degenerated into a patronizing almsgiving, the Welfare State of the future may as easily become depersonalized, a matter of card-indexes, and numbers, thereby losing the individual contact and concern which characterized the voluntary services. It is here that the religious tradition must seek opportunities for continued influence. The Churches should inspire administrators, inspectors, almoners, and other social functionaries with the ideal of the social services as essentially a cure of souls, that is of a personal and individual concern for the beneficiaries. In particular the Free Churches, whose *raison d'être* has been largely their insistence upon the supremacy of the individual conscience, should find no lack of opportunities for this kind of service.

But the menace from the totalitarian despotisms from without is the more serious and far-reaching. For Christianity in its corporate expression through the several Churches is subject to the vicissitudes common to human history; and not least to the threat of forcible suppression by the sword. This lesson indeed is writ large in its own history; for the advance of Islam not only brought to an end some of the most numerous and flourishing Christian Churches in the Middle East and north

Africa, but Christianity has never recovered its former position in these regions. It would be folly to ignore the possibility that the anti-Christian offensive mounted by contemporary totalitarian states may achieve a victory of equal, if not greater, proportions. For in addition to their wielding of a far more formidable armoury than previous despotisms, they are possessed also of hitherto unprecedented means of moulding and fashioning public opinion. Moreover, the challenge to the Christian tradition to-day is world-wide, not local, as the immediate situation in the Far East or in Africa sufficiently illustrates. Inevitably therefore the English religious tradition merges into the ecumenical Christian tradition, contending for victory against the principalities and powers and rulers of world-darkness. Its influence must therefore be judged by its contribution to the world-wide strategy by which alone Christianity can hope to meet a world-wide challenge; and in point of historical fact, it has been the outspreading of the English-speaking peoples which has done much to fashion the present ecumenical movement of Christendom.

It is from this standpoint that the fusion of the missionary expansion of Christianity in the nineteenth century with the twentieth century ecumenical movement constitutes the most significant and important factor of contemporary church history. The maxim of William Carey to expect great things of God together with the ambitious aspiration of the Student Volunteer Movement for Foreign Missions to evangelize the world in this generation, represent the only strategy by which Christianity may hope to rise to the height of its present day vocation. If the Church has become at length, what it has always been in aspiration, Universal it remains for it to realize its unity. To this task it is not unreasonable to hope and expect that the English religious tradition will make its distinctive and influential contribution. Historically, from its loins have sprung episcopalian, presbyterian, and independent Churches which comprise in their world-wide expansion not a little of the Christian forces of to-day. More recently, moreover, the boldest and most promising experiment in ecclesiastical union, the Church of South India, has largely sprung from the coalescence of its several traditions. It is imperative that the greatest possible measure of organic unity and also of co-operation should be attained in face of the challenge of totalitarian systems. 'Comprehension' has became now an ecumenical, not a local, necessity. For a great door and effectual is opened, but there are many adversaries. Alike in the missionary field, in prospect of anti-Christian ideologies abroad, and of secularism at home, there is urgent need of unity.

For though the tired waves, vainly breaking
Seem here no painful inch to gain,
Far back, through creeks and inlets making,
Comes silent, flooding-in, the main.

And not by eastern windows only,
When daylight comes, comes in the light.
In front the sun climbs slow, how slowly,
But, westward, look, the land is bright.

Still, despite storm and tempest and the emergence of new adversaries, *Vexilla Regis prodeunt*, the Royal Banners forward go.

INDEX OF NAMES